IN PRAISE OF THOMAS BUERGENTHAL'S

A LUCKY CHILD

A MEMOIR OF SURVIVING AUSCHWITZ AS A YOUNG BOY

"A gripping memoir.... Thomas Buergenthal's moving story of survival is a testament to the resilience of the human spirit."
—*Jewish Book World*

"In the plainest words and the steadiest tones (as an intimate would speak deadly truth in the dead of night), Thomas Buergenthal delivers to us the child he once was: an unblemished little boy made human prey by Europe's indelible twentieth-century barbarism, a criminality that will never leave off its telling. History and memory fail to ebb; rather, they accelerate and proliferate, and Buergenthal's voice is now more thunderous than ever. Pledged to universal human rights, he has turned a life of gratuitous deliverance into a work of visionary compassion."
—Cynthia Ozick, author of *Heir to the Glimmering World*

"Thomas Buergenthal is not your average misery memoirist. What he has to say, both in bearing witness to the Holocaust and in describing his moral coming-to-adulthood, deserves our attention. His is an extraordinary story and he tells it straight."
—Sam Leith, *Daily Mail*

"Buergenthal's revealing self-portrait provides insight into a career devoted to the international defense of human rights."
— Bonny V. Fetterman, *Reform Judaism Magazine*

"An extraordinary and inspiring book by an extraordinary and inspiring man. It's one of those rare books you devour cover to cover in a single reading. It deserves to be read very widely indeed, especially for anyone desperate for a hint of light in a world that can often seem so very dark."
— Philippe Sands, author of
Torture Team and *Lawless World*

"A remarkable, sometimes astonishing story of finding protection and kindness from unlikely sources, uncanny narrow escapes, and a powerfully strong will to live."
— Betty Gordon, *Atlanta Journal-Constitution*

"Buergenthal is an excellent and evocative storyteller. The fine writing and insights here make this book a powerful choice for teens looking for a mentor through emotional and political challenges of their own."
— Francisca Goldsmith, *School Library Journal*

"What makes this book more important than just another memoir are these important lessons learned. Even if one hasn't 'lived that life' there's much to be learned about the building of character from reading this."
— Christina M. Cerna, International Law
Association Newsletter

"Reminiscent of Anne Frank and Elie Wiesel....Buergenthal speaks most eloquently for the millions of Holocaust victims who cannot." —Mary McReynolds, *Oklahoman*

"This book is one I would have used in my sixth-grade classroom; and it is one I would savor discussing with professional colleagues and personal friends.... How fortunate we are in America that Thomas Buergenthal chose to come here and has dedicated his life to teaching and practicing in the area of human rights."
—Carol Rasco, CEO of Reading Is Fundamental

"Powerful.... The author's story is astonishing and moving, and his capacity for forgiveness is remarkably heartening. An important new voice joins the chorus of survivors."
—*Kirkus Reviews*

"*A Lucky Child* does not wallow in the horrors nor does it shirk the darkest events. It is a clear-headed account of Buergenthal's experiences and how they determined his life."
—Jason Steger, *Sydney Morning Herald*

"A great story of family, love, hope, and survival. Buergenthal calls us to the better angels of our nature."
—Roger Alford, *Opinio Juris*

"The tone is what makes this memoir so rewarding: in the darkness, the indomitable spirit of the child."
—Genevieve Fox, *Daily Telegraph*

A LUCKY CHILD

A MEMOIR OF SURVIVING AUSCHWITZ AS A YOUNG BOY

THOMAS BUERGENTHAL

Foreword by Elie Wiesel

BACK BAY BOOKS
Little, Brown and Company
New York   Boston   London

Back Bay Books / Little, Brown and Company
Hachette Book Group
237 Park Avenue, New York, NY 10017
www.hachettebookgroup.com

Originally published in Germany by Fischer Verlag as *Ein Glückskind*, 2007
First English-language edition published in Great Britain by Profile
Books, February 2009
Published in the U.S. in hardcover by Little, Brown and Company,
April 2009
First Back Bay paperback edition, September 2010

Back Bay Books is an imprint of Little, Brown and Company. The Back
Bay Books name and logo are trademarks of Hachette Book Group, Inc.

Photographs are from the author's collection.
Frontispiece: Thomas during a vacation in Czechoslovakia, 1937
Map on pages xx–xxi courtesy of Peter Palm
Foreword translated from the French by Jesse Browner

Library of Congress Cataloging-in-Publication Data
Buergenthal, Thomas.
  A lucky child : a memoir of surviving Auschwitz as a young boy / Thomas
Buergenthal.
    p. cm.
  ISBN: 978-0-316-04340-3 (HC) / 978-0-316-04339-7 (PB)
    1. Buergenthal, Thomas — Childhood and youth. 2. Jewish children in
the Holocaust — Poland — Personal narratives. 3. World War, 1939–1945 —
Prisoners and prisons, German. 4. Auschwitz (Concentration camp)
5. Holocaust survivors — United States — Biography. I. Title.
    D810.C4B84 2009
    940.53'18092 — dc22   2008033732

15   14   13

RRD-IN

Designed by Greta D. Sibley

Printed in the United States of America

To the memory of my parents,
Mundek and Gerda Buergenthal,
whose love, strength of character,
and integrity inspired this book

Contents

Contents

Foreword

ARE THERE RULES TO HELP A SURVIVOR DECIDE the best
time to bear witness to history? Which is better: to dare to
look directly into the blinding present, no matter how painful, or to await the detachment of hindsight—which, being
less painful, is more objective?

In the literature of what we so inadequately call the
Holocaust, there were prisoners who, possessed by the fear of
oblivion, defied every danger by becoming chroniclers. In the
ghettos and in the death camps, and even in the shadow of
the flames of Birkenau and Treblinka, men scrounged paper
and pencil to write down and preserve their daily existence in
all its appalling horror. These precious documents were discovered buried in the ground or under mountains of ash.

Following the war and shortly after their liberation from
Auschwitz or Buchenwald, some survivors felt the need to
speak out. The world had to be told the truth—not only
about their suffering but also about its own treachery. Others
held their tongues, mostly because they did not have the

strength to relive events that had been just about unbearable. And then too, let us be honest, people preferred not to hear what they had to say. It prevented them from clinging to their own certainties or, more simply, from eating well and sleeping in peace.

Thomas Buergenthal is among those who chose to wait. In his case, the long delay has been rich in human experience. He was already at the height of his career as a professor of law and as a judge before an international court when he decided to revisit his memories.

Is his testimony just one among many, similar to so many others? Well, yes and no. At first glance, all accounts seem to tell the same story. Sometimes we may even wonder whether it was the same German tormentor who abused, tortured, and killed the same Jew six million times. And yet, each story retains its own identity, its own voice.

The voice of the future world court judge strikes us by its need to seek out strains of humanity, even in the very depths of hell.

Kielce, Henryków, Birkenau, Gliwice, and Sachsenhausen —Buergenthal was among the youngest of prisoners in all these places of pain and damnation, where the power of evil and death seemed absolute. Being a mere ten years old in Birkenau made him a rarity, if not almost unique. How did he escape the brutality of the bosses, the agonies of hunger, the fatal diseases, and the selections? More simply put, how did he survive? If he believed in God, he might have evoked divine intervention, but he attributes his survival to luck. As a matter of fact, a clairvoyant had predicted as much to his mother: her son would be lucky. He remembers her saying so.

In the beginning there was the ghetto, with its famished wraiths, its nights of fear, its defeats; profession, wealth, and lineage counted for nothing there. Inside the primal nightmare, a most orderly chaos.

Then, deportation: the nocturnal passage into the unknown. Was it simply by chance that Thomas avoided the scrutiny of the infamous Doctor Mengele upon his arrival at Birkenau? Was there a tangible explanation for his luck? On another occasion, during a selection, the boy was bold enough to announce in German to a commandant that he could work. Amazingly, the commandant pulled him from the group already marked for death. Other boys his age had already gone to "the other place," up there in the clouds, whereas he, Thomas, was still alive. One day, he was astonished to catch a glimpse of his mother in the women's camp.

How can those who have never been put to the test understand how human nature may bend under duress? Why does one man become a pitiless Kapo and victimize an old friend or even his own relative? What makes one man choose to exercise power through cruelty, while another—from exactly the same background—refuses to do so in the name of enfeebled and downtrodden humanity?

Thomas watches, learns, and remembers. Firing squads. Hangings. The prisoner who, not wishing to lose his dignity, kisses the hand of the unfortunate friend condemned to serve as his executioner.

In fact, even in the terrible camp at Sachsenhausen, Thomas finds friends—older than he, men from his own district or from faraway places like Norway—who help him.

Thomas's stories from the days following liberation resemble earlier accounts in their thirst to understand what man, pushed to the very limits, is capable of.

As a child in Göttingen, Germany, he dreamed of going out onto the balcony with a machine gun in his hand to seek vengeance. Later, that dream shamed and humbled him. The same townsmen who, under Hitler, had turned their backs on their Jewish neighbors now embrace them. And Thomas, who has come to Göttingen to be with his mother, does not judge them collectively guilty.

Would he have written the same book fifty years ago? There is no knowing. But he has written it. That alone is what matters. And the reader must surely be thankful to him for it.

—Elie Wiesel

Preface

THIS BOOK SHOULD PROBABLY HAVE BEEN WRITTEN many years ago when the events I describe were still fresh in my mind. But my other life intervened—the life I have lived since I arrived in the United States in 1951, a life filled with educational, professional, and family responsibilities that left little time for the past. It may also be that, without realizing it, I needed the distance of more than half a century to record my earlier life, for it allowed me to look at my childhood experiences with greater detachment and without dwelling on many details that are not really central to the story I now consider important to tell. That story, after all, continues to have a lasting impact on the person I have become.

Of course, I always knew that someday I would tell my story. I had to tell it to my children and then to my grandchildren. I believe that they should know what it was like to be a child in the Holocaust and to have survived the concentration camps. My children had heard snippets of my story at the dinner table and at family gatherings, but it was never the whole story. It is, after all, not a story that lends itself to such occasional telling. But it is a story that must be told and passed on, particularly in a family that was, for all practical purposes, wiped out in the Holocaust. Only thus can the link between the past and the future be reestablished for our family. For example, I never really managed to tell my children, in the proper context, how my parents behaved during the war and the strength of character they displayed at a time when other people under similar circumstances lost their moral compass. The story of their courage and integrity enriches the history of our family, and it must not be allowed to be buried with me.

I also wanted to recount my story to a wider audience, not because I think that my early life was all that noteworthy in the grand scheme of things, but because I have long believed that the Holocaust cannot be fully understood unless we look at it through the eyes of those who lived through it. To speak of the Holocaust in terms of numbers — six million — which is the way it is usually done, is to unintentionally dehumanize the victims and to trivialize the profoundly human tragedy it was. The numbers transform the victims into a fungible mass of nameless, soulless bodies rather than treating them as the individual human beings they were. Each of us who lived through the Holocaust has a personal story worth telling, if only because it puts a human face on the experience. Like all tragedies, the Holocaust produced heroes and villains, ordinary human beings who never lost their humanity and those who, to save themselves or for a mere piece of bread, helped send others to the gas chambers. It is also the story of some

Germans who, in the midst of the carnage, did not lose their humanity.

For me, the individual story of each Holocaust survivor is a valuable addition to the history of the Holocaust. It deepens our understanding of this cataclysmic event that destroyed forever not only European Jewry as such but also its unique culture and character. That is why I tried to write my story as I remember living it as the child I was, not as an old man reflecting on that life. The latter approach would have deprived the story of its character as the contemporaneous personal testimony of one child-survivor of the Holocaust.

This book contains my recollections of events that took place more than six decades ago. These recollections, I am sure, are colored by the tricks that the passage of time and old age play on memory: forgotten or inaccurate names of people; muddled facts and dates of events that took place either earlier or later than recounted; and references to events that did not happen quite as I describe them or that I believe I witnessed but may have only heard about. Because I did not write this book sooner, I could not consult those survivors who were with me in the camps or compare my recollections of specific events with theirs, and that I regret very much. Most of all, I regret that I could not discuss the details with my mother. Also, despite my best efforts, I have found it difficult, if not impossible, particularly in the book's first two chapters, to distinguish clearly between some events I actually remember witnessing and those I was told about by my parents or overheard them discuss. All I can say is that as I wrote about them, I seemed to remember them clearly as firsthand experiences.

Although the chapters of this book are organized in chronological order, I have not necessarily recounted the individual events or episodes in that same order within the chapters. After all these years, I can recall particular events or episodes, frequently very clearly, but not exactly when they occurred. To the child I was, dates and time had no significance. As I try to recall that period of my life, I realize that I did not think in terms of days, months, or even years, as I would today. I grew up in the camps — I knew no other life — and my sole objective was to stay alive, from hour to hour, from day to day. That was my mind-set. I measured time only in terms of the hours we had to wait to receive our next meal or the days remaining before Dr. Mengele would most likely mount another of his deadly selections. Thus, for example, when starting to write this book, I had no idea when in 1944 I arrived in Auschwitz. I obtained that information only after consulting the Auschwitz archives. The Internet provided me with the date of the liquidation of the Ghetto of Kielce and that of my liberation from Sachsenhausen. This is the extent of my research for the book; the rest of the story I tell is based on my own recollections.

Had I written this book in the mid-1950s, when I made a first attempt to tell part of my story by publishing an account of the Auschwitz death march in a college literary magazine, this memoir would have conveyed a greater sense of immediacy. Unencumbered by the mellowing impact that the passage of time has on memory, particularly painful memories, I could then still clearly recall my fear of dying, the hunger I experienced, the sense of loss and insecurity that gripped me on being separated from my parents, and my reactions to the horrors I witnessed. The passage of time and the life I have lived since the Holocaust have dulled those feelings and emotions. As the author of this book, I regret that for I am sure that the reader would have been interested in that part of the story as well. But I am convinced that if these feelings and emotions had stayed with me all these years, I might have found it difficult to overcome my Holocaust past without serious psychological scars. It may have been my salvation that these memories faded away over time.

My Holocaust experience has had a very substantial impact on the human being I have become, on my life as an international law professor, human rights lawyer, and international judge. It might seem obvious that my past would draw me to human rights and to international law, whether or not I knew it at the time. In any event, it equipped me to be a better human rights lawyer, if only because I understood, not only intellectually but also emotionally, what it is like to be a victim of human rights violations. I could, after all, feel it in my bones.

A LUCKY
CHILD

CHAPTER 1

From Lubochna to Poland

IT WAS JANUARY 1945. Our open railroad cars offered little protection against the cold, the wind, and the snow so typical of the harsh winters of eastern Europe. We were crossing Czechoslovakia on our way from Auschwitz in Poland to the Sachsenhausen concentration camp in Germany. As our train approached a bridge spanning the railroad tracks, I saw people waving at us from above, and then, suddenly, loaves of bread came raining down on us. The bread kept coming as we passed under one or two more bridges. Except for snow, I had eaten nothing since we had boarded the train at the end of a three-day forced march out of Auschwitz, only a few days ahead of the advancing Soviet troops. The bread probably saved my life and that of many others who were with me on what came to be known as the Auschwitz Death Transport.

At the time, it did not occur to me to connect the bread from the bridges with Czechoslovakia, the country of my birth. That came years after the war, usually on those occasions when, for one reason or another, I was asked to present a birth certificate. Since I did not have one, I would be required to provide an affidavit, attesting—"on information and belief"—that I was born in Lubochna, Czechoslovakia, on May 11, 1934. Whenever I signed one of these documents, I would invariably have a flashback to those bridges in Czechoslovakia.

Not long after the Communist regime collapsed in Czechoslovakia in December of 1989, I finally managed to obtain my birth certificate. It confirmed what I had claimed in my many affidavits and provided the impetus for a visit by my wife, Peggy, and me to Lubochna—she out of curiosity to see where I was born, and I in order to connect with that one piece of land on earth where I first opened my eyes.

We reached Lubochna, a small resort town in the lower Tatra Mountains in today's Slovakia, after driving for a few hours on winding roads, alongside noisy brooks and meandering rivers, from Bratislava, its capital. Without having planned it, we arrived in Lubochna in May 1991, almost fifty-seven years to the day of my birth there. A beautifully sunny day greeted us as we drove into this small town surrounded by the inviting, mellow mountains, which distinguish the lower Tatras from the harsher high Tatras.

Now I understood why my father had dreamed of one day coming back to Lubochna and why my mother had loved it here. It seemed such an idyllic place. As Peggy and I walked through the town in the hope of finding what used to be my parents' hotel, I realized that but for the official-looking piece of paper that forever linked me to Lubochna, nothing else did. We never found the hotel—I later learned that it had been demolished sometime in the 1960s. Although my visit confirmed to me that Lubochna was truly the beautiful place my parents frequently talked about, I realized with considerable sadness that for my family and me this town represented little more than a historical footnote in a story that began here with the joy brought on by the birth of a child, a story that gradually gave way to what became a very different tale.

My father, Mundek Buergenthal, had moved to Lubochna from Germany shortly before Hitler came to power in 1933. Together with friend Erich Godal, an anti-Nazi political cartoonist working for a major Berlin daily, he decided to open a small hotel in Lubochna, where Godal owned some property. The political situation in Germany was becoming ever more perilous for Jews and for those who opposed Hitler and the ideology of his Nazi party. My father and Godal apparently believed that Germany's enthusiasm for Hitler would wane in a few years and that they would then be able to return to Berlin. In the meantime, the proximity of Czechoslovakia to Germany would allow them to follow developments there more closely and enable them to provide temporary refuge to any of their friends who might need to leave Germany in a hurry.

My father was born in 1901 in Galicia, a region of Poland that belonged to the Austro-Hungarian Empire before the First World War. German and Polish were the languages in which he received his primary and much of his secondary school education. His parents lived in a village on a farm that belonged to a wealthy Polish landowner whose extensive agricultural estate was administered by my paternal grandfather,

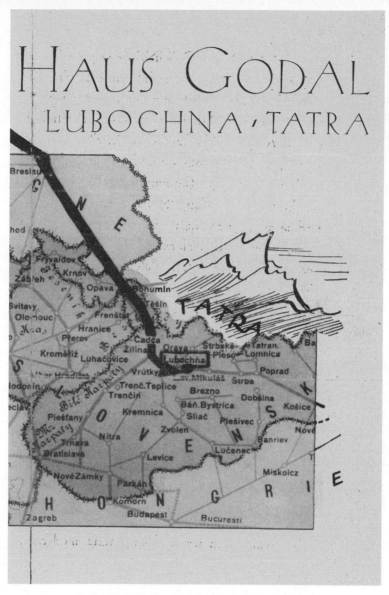

HAUS GODAL
LUBOCHNA · TATRA

Pages from the hotel prospectus of Haus Godal,
the Buergenthal family hotel in Lubochna

STAATSBAD LUBOCHNA, das slowakische Karlsbad, liegt 600 m hoch traumhaft schön in den dichten Gebirgswäldern der Tatra, umgeben von einem romantischen Kranz 12–1500 m hoher Berge. Man erreicht Lubochna in elf stündiger D=Zug=Faht ab Berlin über Breslau = Oderberg (Bohumin). Ab 15. Mai ist es D=Zug=Station. Lu= bochna gehört noch nicht zu den Kur= orten, in denen sich der lärmende Betrieb der Großstadt fortsetzt. Alles ist zu absoluter Erho= lung geschaffen: die herrlicheGe= birgs=Waldluft, das mildeKlima, die tiefe Ruhe des Gebirgs= tales.

Zwischen Kur= haus und Post, völlig zentral liegt das HAUS GODAL, in einem herrlichen 12000 qm großen Garten. Es ist ein Landhaus mit 18 Zimmern Alle Fremdenzimmer sind mit ganz modernen niedrigen farbigen Lackmöbeln eingerichtet, jedes Zimmer hat fließendes warmes und kaltes Wasser. — Die Mahlzeiten werden auf der 22 m langen Glasveranda eingenommen, die dem Gebirge zu=

gewandt liegt.— Der Garten hat Liegewiesen, für jeden Gast ist ein Liegestuhl vorgesehen.

Besonderer Wert ist auf die Ver= pflegung gelegt, die absolut erst= klassig ist und nach deutsch=böhmischer Art zubereitet wird. Der Speisezettel eines Tages sieht ungefähr so aus:

Frühstück: 2 Eier oder Aufschnitt ‹ Butter, Konfitüren, Gebäck, Kaffee, Tee oder Kakao nach Wahl.

Mittag: Suppe od. Pastete, 1 Fleischgang mit Ge= müse, Früchte od. Kompott, Süßspeise, Mokka.

Abends: 1 warmer Fleischgang, Käseplatte oder Früchte.

Pages from the hotel prospectus of Haus Godal, the Buergenthal family hotel in Lubochna an unusual occupation for a Jew at that time in that part of the world. The Polish landowner had been my grandfather's commanding officer in the Austrian army and took him into his service when they both returned to private life. Eventually, he put my grandfather in charge of his many farms.

The nearest high school my father could attend was located in a town some distance away. Family lore has it that, to get to that school, my father boarded for a time at the home of the flagman in charge of a strategically located railroad crossing. Trains going to and from that town would pass the crossing a few times a day. Since there was no train station nearby, the flagman would slow down the train in the morning and then again in the afternoon to enable my father to jump on and off. Later, less hazardous arrangements were made for him to attend school.

After graduating from high school and a brief stint in the Polish army during the Russo-Polish War that began in 1919, my father enrolled in the law school of the University of Krakow. Before completing his studies, however, he left Poland and moved to Berlin. There he joined his older sister, who was married to a well-known Berlin couturier, and obtained a job with a private Jewish bank. He rose rapidly through the ranks, becoming an officer of the bank at a relatively young age due to his success in helping to manage the bank's investment portfolio. His position at the bank and his brother-in-law's social contacts enabled him to meet many writers, journalists, and actors living in Berlin. The rise of Hitler and the ever-increasing attacks by his followers on Jews and anti-Nazi intellectuals, quite a number of whom were friends of my father, prompted him to leave Germany and settle in Lubochna.

Gerda Silbergleit, my mother, or Mutti to me, arrived at my father's hotel in 1933. She came from Göttingen, the German university town where she was born and where her parents owned a shoe store. Not quite twenty-one years old at the time — she was born in 1912 — her parents had sent her to Lubochna in the hope that a vacation in Czechoslovakia would help her get over the non-Jewish boyfriend who wanted to marry her. They also thought that it would be good for their daughter to leave Göttingen for a while. There, the harassment of Jews — and, in particular, of young Jewish women — by Nazi youths roaming the streets was making life increasingly more unpleasant for her.

When making arrangements for my mother's stay at the hotel, her parents asked that she be met at the German-Czech border. Instead of sending his driver, my father decided to drive alone to the border, where he gave her the impression that he was the hotel's chauffeur. She was quite embarrassed when at dinner she was seated at the table of the hotel's owner, who turned out to be the driver she had quizzed about Mr. Buergenthal, whom her mother had described as a very eligible bachelor. Years later, whenever I heard my mother tell this story, I wondered whether her visit to Lubochna had been arranged by her parents, in part at least with a possible marriage to my father in mind, and whether, if there were such a plan, my father was in on it. Was it just a coincidence that his hotel was recommended to my grandparents by a friend who also knew my father well? I never did get the whole

Gerda and Mundek Buergenthal, circa 1933

story, assuming there was more to it. To my mother, it was always love at first sight, and that was it!

My parents were engaged three days after they met at the German-Czech border. They were married a few weeks later, but not until my maternal grandfather, Paul Silbergleit,

Thomas with his parents, May 1937

and then my grandmother, Rosa Silbergleit née Blum, had traveled to Lubochna to pass judgment on the bridegroom. They were apparently somewhat taken aback by the rapidity of the engagement and the prospect of a hasty marriage, but it was 1933, and there was little time for courting. I was born some eleven months later. By 1939 we were refugees on the run, only a few steps ahead of the Germans. A whole country, it seemed, had declared war on a family of three whose only crime was that they were Jews.

As I search my memory for some aspects of my brief life in Lubochna, I have a hard time separating what my parents told me from what I actually remember. My guess is that much of what I think I remember from that period I actually heard later from either my father or my mother. My mother frequently recalled that at the age of three or four I served as her interpreter when she went shopping in Slovakia. She spoke only German and the shopkeepers for the most part only Slovak. I could apparently get along in both languages. We spoke German at home when the three of us were together, and I must have picked up Slovak from my Slovak nannies.

My only clear recollection of life in Lubochna dates back to a day in late 1938 or early 1939 when my parents told me that we had to leave our hotel. As they began to pack our belongings, they appeared to be very much in a hurry. Years later, I was told that the Hlinka Guard, a Slovak fascist party supported by Nazi Germany that controlled Slovakia, had claimed to have had a court order declaring a group close to it the owner of our hotel (my parents had purchased Erich

Thomas leaning on a fence, Czechoslovakia, 1937

Godal's share in the hotel some years earlier). There was no way to successfully challenge this confiscation of our hotel. By that time, the Hlinka Guard and its followers controlled the courts, and their police threatened to expel us from the country if we resisted their takeover or failed to leave Lubochna immediately.

As a result, we could take only a few suitcases with us, leaving everything else, in addition to the hotel itself, to the new "owners." But I wanted my car to come with us! It was a little red car with pedals. I was told I could not take it along but that we would soon be back and that it would be waiting for me on our return. That car was my most treasured possession. I must have sensed that I would never see it again, for I went to the storeroom to look for it. There it was, propped up on its rear wheels, leaning against a post, surrounded by boxes and suitcases. It looked as sad as I felt. To this day, when I think back to that moment, I can still see my little red car.

After leaving Lubochna, we lived for a time in Zilina, also in Slovakia. At first, we stayed with friends who owned the Grand Hotel in that city. I remember the name because I had a wonderful time standing at its main entrance with one of the doormen and, as was then the custom, calling out "Grand Hotel!" to passersby. They would frequently engage me in conversation and, to my delight, sometimes even tossed me a small coin.

From the hotel, we moved to a small apartment in Zilina. Here, my mother and I were often alone. My father had found a job as a traveling salesman for a medical instrument company and spent a lot of time visiting customers in different parts of the country. My parents had apparently used most of their savings, including the money my mother had received from her parents as dowry, to enlarge the hotel in Lubochna and to buy out their former partner. Now the hotel was gone and with it the income they had depended on.

The red car, Thomas's favorite toy, 1937

While we lived in Lubochna, Mutti had never had to cook. That was done by the hotel's chef, a massive and intimidating Slovak matron, who let my father know in no uncertain terms that his young wife was not welcome in her kitchen. Now, in Zilina, things were different, and I soon realized that my mother was not a very good cook. Once she roasted a chicken without cleaning its insides very well. When my father started to eat it, he ended up with a mouthful of corn, which must have been the remains of the chicken's last meal. Of course, he spat it all out, and they had a big fight, with my father yelling, "I thought they taught you something at that finishing school in Göttingen!" She counterattacked by reminding him of some long-forgotten incident for which he was supposedly to blame. And when he replied that that had nothing to do with her bad cooking, she accused him of changing the subject. I soon realized that she would always win these arguments, while he would end up shaking his head in utter disbelief. At times she would also make me her coconspirator when she did something she did not want my father to know. Once, when she realized that the kitchen rag she had been looking for had fallen into the pot in which she happened to be cooking, she swore me to secrecy and assured me, "Papa will not notice anything if we don't tell."

One day, while my father was out of town, the police came to our apartment and ordered my mother to pack our belongings and make sure that we would be ready to go with them within the hour. We were Jews and undesirable foreigners, we were told, and were being expelled from the country. My mother protested that we could not leave without my father

*The Buergenthal family, already on
the run—Slovakia, circa 1938*

but to no avail. We were taken to the police station. Its building and courtyard were already filled with other foreigners. My mother recognized some of our friends among them. People were sitting on their suitcases, children were crying, and I sensed that everybody was very afraid, just as I was.

As soon as we arrived at the police station, my mother, in her precise, clipped German, demanded to see the chief of police or the person in charge. She made a tremendous amount of noise while waving a leather-bound document with a lot of stamps on it. After a few minutes, we were taken into an office. Here a heavyset man in uniform, who was not very friendly, asked in a threatening tone of voice what all the commotion was about and who she thought she was. My mother, who seemed very tall to me at that moment, but who measured slightly less than five feet, slammed her document on the man's desk and barked at him in German: "We are Germans!" Pointing to the document on the desk, which she called her passport, she continued in that same tone: "We are supposed to be your allies! It is an outrage that you are treating us like common criminals." She immediately wanted to be taken to the German consul to protest this scandalous treatment, and she warned the police official that he and his superiors were going to be in very serious trouble from the German authorities for harassing Germans living peacefully in Slovakia. "Just you wait and see what will happen when my husband comes back and does not find us at home!"

After a whispered conversation with another man and some further inspection of the passport, the officer suddenly smiled at us, got up from behind his desk, grasped my mother's hand, and, in broken German, apologized to her profusely. This was all a big mistake; of course they were not deporting Germans living in Slovakia, only foreign Jews and other undesirables who should not have been allowed into the country in the first place. He shook my mother's hand again, saluted, and ordered a policeman to escort us home.

Years later, I learned that my mother's "passport" was in fact a German driver's license, which looked like a passport. Her German passport had been confiscated when she tried to renew it because, like other Jews living abroad, she had apparently been stripped of her German citizenship. To this day, I wonder what she would have done had the police officer been able to read German and called her bluff. The last person she wanted to talk to at that moment was the German consul.

I continue to marvel at the courage, ingenuity, and intelligence my mother demonstrated that day, character traits she was to reveal many times over in the future, under even more difficult circumstances. Where did this young woman from a well-to-do, protective, Jewish middle-class home with barely a secondary school education derive the cunning and almost reckless gall to assess and take advantage of the weakness of those posing a serious threat to her or her family and come out the winner? As a child, I assumed that it was only natural for my mother to always know what to do. But what was then "natural" has continued over the years to inspire my profound admiration and to puzzle me, not only because she repeatedly succeeded in beating the odds when confronting the Nazi killing machine, but also because she seemed to pull off these successes at a moment's notice with the speed of a magician. Where did that magic come from? Although I have tried, I have never quite been able to identify the intellectual and emotional source of my mother's special gift. All I know is that she had it.

As soon as we had returned to our apartment from the police station, Mutti exclaimed, "We were lucky this time!" But then she added, "They will be back," and began looking for my father's handgun. He had acquired it in Lubochna to scare off foxes and other animals that sometimes tried to get into the chicken coop behind the hotel's woodshed. When my mother found the gun, she told me that we had to throw it away secretly so that the police would not find it the next time they came. She handled the gun very gingerly, let it slide into a paper bag, and told me not to touch it. The next day, we walked to the river and threw the gun into the water from one of the bridges. I did not understand it but felt very grown up to be participating in this highly secret operation. When my father returned, he was very angry to learn that my mother had thrown his gun away, but it was too late to do anything about it.

A few days later, my parents decided that Slovakia was no longer safe for us and that the time had come to leave. They expected the harassment of Jews, particularly foreign Jews, to become more severe in that part of Czechoslovakia. My father was also afraid that he was on a Gestapo "Wanted" list, and if the police were to come back, they might arrest him and turn him over to the Germans. But where could we go? That was a question I heard my parents discuss over and over again in whispered tones, usually at night when I was supposed to be asleep. Eventually, they settled on Poland. It was the only country they thought we might be allowed to enter. There, moreover, my father would be able to obtain the visas that he had been promised by the British authorities in Czechoslovakia and that would allow us to travel to England as political refugees.

Soon we were on our way to Poland. It took us a while to get very far, however, since we were trapped in the no-man's-land between Poland and Czechoslovakia. This strip of land measured some fifty yards from border post to border post. The borders were connected by a dirt road that cut through a field. On either side of the road ran a deep drainage ditch. The Polish border post was at one end of the road, the Czech at the other. As soon as we got to the Polish side of the border, the Polish guards would order us back to the Czech side. The Czechs, in turn, would not allow us to reenter. And so it went for days. To me, the strip of road seemed much longer than it probably was because of the many times we had to move from one end to the other, carrying or pushing our suitcases while the border guards kept yelling at us not to show up again.

We must have been stateless and have had no valid travel documents. My father probably lost his Polish citizenship under a Polish law, enacted in 1938, which stripped all Poles of their citizenship if they remained outside the country for more than five years. I do not know whether he had earlier acquired German citizenship, but if he had, he would have lost it, as my mother did, when the Nazis denaturalized Jews living abroad. As stateless persons, once in no-man's-land we had no right to enter Poland or to return to Czechoslovakia. Every day and every night, my father would wait for the guards to change shifts on the Polish side of the border. As soon as he saw new Polish guards there, he would march us up to the guardhouse and ask to be admitted, claiming that he was a Pole. But since he lacked the necessary papers to prove it, the guards would order us to return to the Czech side. Back and forth we went, day and night. We would sleep in the field adjacent to the road between the border posts or in one of the ditches. On rare occasions, we would be allowed to sleep in the waiting room of one of the guardhouses. While we were cold most of the time, we were not hungry because the Czech or Polish farmers would sell us bread and sausages. But we were not going very far. I was tired and did not understand why nobody wanted to let us into their country.

A week or so after we had first arrived at the border, on a day when we had again been ordered by the Poles to return to the Czech side and just as we were dragging our belongings toward that side, we were met by heavily armed German soldiers. It seems that Germany had occupied Czechoslovakia, and here we were, in the clutches of the very people we were trying to escape. I could sense that my parents were very afraid. One of the Germans, who appeared to be in charge, wanted to know who we were and what we were doing in the middle of nowhere. My father, who suddenly spoke very poor German, answered that we were Poles, that we had been here for more than a week, and that the Poles would not allow us to return to our country. "We shall see about that," snarled the German officer. With those words, he ordered two of his soldiers to come over and pick up our suitcases. I thought that they were going to do something terrible to us, because my mother suddenly grasped my hand very tightly and stopped me from speaking. But the German soldiers merely walked us back to the Polish border. Once there, they ordered the Polish border guards to let us pass. "These people are Poles!" yelled one of the soldiers. "I order you to let them in. You had better not send them to our side again. Things are going to be different from now on!" My father translated what the German was saying, and the Poles nodded obediently.

That is how we got into Poland. It must have been March of 1939, for that is when Germany marched into Czechoslovakia. I was almost five years old.

CHAPTER 2

Katowice

I HAVE NO RECOLLECTION OF THE FIRST DAYS after we were
finally allowed to cross into Poland. We must have stayed in a
boardinghouse or a rented room for a short while, and I must
have slept much of the time. My first memory is of the three
of us sitting in a horse-drawn hay wagon with our suitcases
piled up at one end. The driver was an old man with a long
white beard. He wore a black hat and spoke with my father
in a language that sounded German but which I could barely
understand. These were the first Yiddish words I had ever
heard, and he was the first Hasidic Jew I had ever seen. I
can still hear the driver say something about "a shoo," which
at the time made we wonder why he spoke of a *Schuh* (the
German word for shoe). Only much later, when I picked up
Yiddish from my playmates in the Ghetto of Kielce, did I
realize that "a shoo" meant an hour in Yiddish and that the
driver had told my father that it would take about an hour for
us to reach our destination.

Our next stop was Warsaw. Here my father had some relatives, and since my mother had never met any of them, we were greeted by them with much rejoicing and kissing, lots of laughter, and enormous amounts of food. I hated these visits because all the women kept kissing me and stuffing me with food. Fortunately, there were always some children around with whom I could escape from the grown-ups and play.

These visits came to an end when I caught a severe case of whooping cough from one of my playmates. The doctor told my parents that inhaling river air would do wonders for me. To my delight, my parents acted almost immediately on the doctor's recommendation and hired a horse-drawn carriage to drive me back and forth across a bridge over the Vistula River that connected Warsaw with Praga, its eastern suburb. I loved these daily excursions and was very sad when my cough gradually subsided and my parents decided that we could leave Warsaw and travel to Katowice.

By 1939, Katowice, a city in the southern part of Poland, had become a gathering point for German Jewish refugees. Here they registered with the British consulate in the hope of obtaining the necessary documents allowing them to travel to England. My parents had been told in Warsaw that the British consulate in Katowice would handle our visa applications, and that the sooner we got there the sooner we would be able to leave for England. My whooping cough had delayed our arrival in Katowice.

In Katowice we moved into a small apartment. I'll never forget our first night in that apartment. My parents had barely turned off the lights when the room we shared seemed to come alive. My mother screamed that she was being bitten to death. When my father jumped out of bed and switched on the light, we found the walls of the room and our beds covered with bedbugs. They were crawling all over us. It was quite a sight to behold: there seemed to be hundreds of ugly orange yellow bugs, and their vicious bites itched intolerably.

My mother wanted to leave right away, but my father calmed her down and explained to her that we were lucky to have this place. Once they had convinced themselves that we had no choice but to stay, my parents mounted a veritable bedbug extermination campaign. They found some candles and began to burn the bugs off the walls; they shook them out of the sheets and stepped on them on the floor. There was a sink in the room, and my mother started shaking the bedbugs from the sheets into the sink in the hope of drowning them. These desperate efforts to rid us of bedbugs must have gone on all night. I fell asleep after a while without realizing that bedbugs would be the least of our problems in the years ahead.

I had a lot of fun in Katowice. There the refugees formed their own little community. My parents became part of it and soon made many friends in this group. As was customary in Germany, these friends immediately became my "uncles" and "aunts." I played with their children, and they kept an eye on me when my parents had to be away on an errand. They usually gathered in some café or park. Here they played cards, read newspapers, whispered a lot about the war that was coming, and worried. Everybody was waiting for their "lucky day." And every so often, there would be a celebration, much kissing, and many tears: somebody's lucky day had arrived in the form of a long-awaited visa from the British consulate, allowing the recipient to travel to England. Soon those who had been granted visas would leave Katowice, usually in small groups or transports put together by the British consulate.

Our lucky day was not to come for some time. In the meantime, I remember playing in a lovely park in Katowice and swimming in a nearby lake. The Jewish community in the city apparently provided some help for needy refugees, as did various individuals associated with it. I remember being taken shopping by a very nice man who had befriended my parents and returning home with toys and wearing a completely new outfit: new pants, shirt, and jacket. He had thought I looked too German in the clothes my mother liked me to wear. From time to time, we would also be invited to dinner in Jewish homes, although this did not happen all that often, and certainly not as often as I would have liked; I would have been happy to escape our ugly room and meager meals.

One day my mother came home in a very excited state. She told my father that she and a girlfriend had gone to a famous fortune-teller. Before going in, Mutti had taken off her wedding ring, and, because she looked much younger than her age—she was twenty-seven years old at the time—she was very surprised when the fortune-teller, after studying her cards, proclaimed that my mother was married and had one child. In addition to knowing a great deal about our family background, the fortune-teller told my mother that her son was *"ein Glückskind"* — a lucky child — and that he would emerge unscathed from the future that awaited us.

My father scolded my mother for believing this nonsense and for spending money on it when we had barely any left. But my mother claimed that her girlfriend had paid for the visit because she wanted someone to accompany her. "Besides, maybe the fortune-teller knows something we don't know, for how else could she have known so much about me?" she retorted. "The only thing the fortune-teller knows that we don't know is how to make money in these bad times," barked my father. The argument between them continued for a while.

None of us knew at the time, and I only found out much later, that the fortune-teller's prediction about me would sustain my mother's hopes in the years ahead, when we were separated. Even after the war, when friends tried to convince her to give up searching for me and not to continue torturing herself, for "Tommy could not possibly have survived," she would reply that she knew I was alive. To me, she insisted years later that everything the fortune-teller had told her had come true. "Of course, I don't believe in this hocus-pocus," she would add in all earnestness, only to contradict herself immediately by asking, "but how do you explain that she was right about you and me?"

Our lucky day came a few weeks after my mother's visit to the fortune-teller. We received the prized visas for travel to England and were scheduled to leave Katowice on September 1, 1939. There was the usual excitement among our friends, with everybody wishing us well and expressing the hope that we would all soon be reunited in England. I was told that we would be in England in a few weeks and that once there we would no longer have to be afraid of the Nazis.

But it was not to be. On our "lucky day," Hitler decided to invade Poland. When we arrived at the Katowice railroad station, where our transport was to be put together, the people from the British consulate told us that it was no longer possible to leave from a Polish port. Arrangements had therefore been made to get us to England via the Balkans. Despite the onrush of people who were trying to leave Katowice that morning, probably because it was not far from the German border, we eventually got to board the railroad car that had been reserved for us and for some other refugees who had also received their visas. Finally, after a long delay, the train moved out of the station. We seemed to have made it.

I don't know how long we traveled on that train. For the most part, though, the train was stopped more than it moved, waiting for other trains loaded with soldiers to pass. The roads along the railroad lines were crowded with people walking or riding in horse-drawn carriages and wagons. Everywhere there were long columns of soldiers, marching and on horseback and in trucks, pulling artillery pieces and supplies. The soldiers were moving toward the front in the direction opposite that of the civilians, who had to make room for them to pass, not always an easy task on the narrow roads.

For me, all this commotion was very exciting. I spent much time waving to the passing soldiers and admiring their uniforms and three-cornered hats. And then, suddenly, the fun stopped. Our train had again halted, this time next to a Polish military train. That train was filled with soldiers and military equipment. On each side of the tracks were open fields. We had probably not been there for more than a few minutes when we began to hear the far-off sounds of approaching airplanes. Then they were above us—two or three planes. People began to scream, *"Niemcy! Niemcy!"* ("Germans! Germans!"), and the air resounded with the rattle of machine-gun fire and the thump of exploding bombs. The train began to shake. The noise was terrible.

My father grabbed my mother and me and pushed us out of the train. "They are attacking the military train!" he screamed above the noise. "We must get out, we must get out." Some people had already jumped from the train and were scrambling across the tracks into the fields. We followed them, pushed on by others. The Polish soldiers began to shoot at the German planes with rifles held out of their train's windows. They did not have much luck. The planes kept swooping down on the trains and the railroad tracks, blowing up some of the carriages. They kept repeating this maneuver for what seemed like a very long time.

Once we managed to get to the nearby field, my mother threw herself on top of me while my father shielded both of us with his body. People were screaming as the planes flew over us with their machine guns blazing. They could easily have killed all of us, but it seemed we were not their targets. Then, just as suddenly as they had appeared, the planes were gone. We waited for a while for them to return, and when they did not, we got up and started to look around. No one on our side of the field seemed to have been hit, but people were wailing, and a few children were crying. Some railroad cars were on fire; there was smoke everywhere. Many injured and dead soldiers were lying on the other side of the tracks and near their train. The tracks had been destroyed as far as the eye could see.

After a while, my father went to look for our belongings. He found some bags and dragged them back to the field. Here we were soon joined by others from our group. "What now?" was the question being asked, and "Where are we?" Nobody seemed to have any answers, and except for my father, no one in the group spoke Polish. He soon learned from some passing farmers that we were not far from Sandomierz, a town some two hundred kilometers east of Katowice.

We stayed overnight in a barn, and then our little group began the trek east to the Russian border, sometimes in hired horse-drawn wagons and other times on foot. The roads were teeming with civilians and soldiers. Like us, most of the civilians were trying to get away from the invading Germans. Every day there were more people on the road. We slept in open fields or in barns and made little progress in our move east. The farmers would charge us for the use of their barns and sell us food. Often, the barns would already be rented out by the time we got there, and then we would have to sleep outside. Some farmers were kind to us; others were not. The latter frequently called us bad names. Here I first learned that we were *"Parzywe Zydzi"* — Scabby Jews.

There were rumors that German spies were everywhere. My father heard that the public was being warned by the

Polish government to be on the lookout for German spies. Our little group was suspect because, except for my father, its members spoke only German. With increasing frequency, my father would have to explain who we were and show our English travel documents to suspicious Polish officials. After a while, only he would go out to the villages to buy food for our group and to get the latest news. I would sometimes accompany him. There we would listen to a radio or talk to the farmers. The information we would bring back seemed always to be the same: "Things don't look too good. The Germans are advancing; the Polish army is retreating."

Every so often, my father would speak with somebody who had recently come back from Russia or had news from there. Here too, the story was usually the same. "Terrible things are happening in that country. Not a good place for foreigners; many of them are being sent to Siberia." Nobody in our group wanted to believe these reports since we had hoped to escape to Russia. Finally, my father decided to see for himself; we were not very far from the Polish-Russian border. He was back a few days later and announced that it would be better to take our chances in Poland. I don't know whether he had actually crossed into Russia or whether he had spoken to people at the border, but he was convinced that it would be a mistake for us to try to get into Russia. "Conditions are terrible," he reported, "particularly for foreigners. A lot of people are getting arrested or deported. The lucky ones are turned back at the border."

"If not Russia, then what?" somebody asked, prompting a long and often heated discussion about the fate that awaited us in a Poland under German occupation. It continued into the night. When I woke up the next morning, the decision had been made. Instead of seeking to enter Russia, we would try to reach Kielce, a city west of Sandomierz with a large Jewish community that might take us in.

Little had changed on the roads. They were even more congested. We were being stopped often and asked to produce our papers. At times, there were tense moments as my father tried to convince Polish military officers that we were not German spies. The news from the front was not very good, my father told us. It was getting worse every day. The Poles were blaming German spies for their military setbacks and the rapid German advances.

My father tried to cheer everybody up by telling us that we would soon be in Kielce and sleeping in real beds again. That was great news for me, but it had little effect on the grim mood that had gripped our little group. I heard someone say that we did not have much to look forward to. "We will either be shot by the Poles as spies or by the Nazis because we are Jews. What is better?" one of my adopted uncles asked with a grin, and everybody laughed. After a while, though, nothing seemed to be funny anymore.

A few days after our decision to walk to Kielce, we began to hear what sounded like a distant thunderstorm. "Artillery fire," my father told me, "but it is far away from here. Listen." And he showed me how, by lying down and pressing my ear to the ground, I would be able to hear it much better. I had a lot of fun playing this game. More and more Polish soldiers and their equipment could be seen on the road and in nearby fields. After a while, the entire road was taken up by retreating troops, at which point all civilians were ordered off the road. We waited and rested in a ditch nearby. It seemed to take hours before the last of the Polish soldiers had passed. Then suddenly, we heard the roar of approaching engines and saw walls of dust in the distance. "Tanks! German tanks!" I could almost touch the fear that swept over our little group. But then I heard my father's reassuring voice, "Stay calm! Don't anybody run! Don't say anything unless spoken to."

As the tanks approached — they advanced toward us on the road and across the fields — we were enveloped in dust and smoke. One of the tanks stopped near our group, and a young soldier, his body protruding from the open turret, his face covered in soot, yelled over to us in German, wanting to know who we were. After some hesitation, somebody answered that we were Jews, and another added, "German Jews." "Nothing to worry about," he yelled back. "The war will be over soon, and we'll all be able to go home again." He waved at us and the tank moved forward. These very reassuring words brought us temporary relief. People began to joke and laugh again. But as fate would have it, they turned out to be the kindest words any German would address to us for a long time to come.

Notwithstanding what the young soldier had said, for us the war had really only just begun. We continued toward Kielce. Near Opatów, some thirty kilometers west of Sandomierz, a wealthy Polish farmer allowed us to stay in one of his barns. He and my father would go off to talk for hours at a time. My mother would always worry until my father returned, and then the two of them would whisper a lot. I later learned that the farmer and some of his friends were in the process of forming a Polish resistance group to fight the Germans. They wanted my father to join them; they needed people who spoke German and Polish and had military experience. We would not have to worry about food or a place to stay, and a way would be found to get us false identification papers. My father and mother talked about this offer for days. Eventually, my father turned it down. They were both very sad that they had to make this decision. The problem was that my father and I, because of our features and light hair color, could have passed for Poles. But my mother spoke no Polish, and her wavy dark hair and brown eyes would have given her away as a Jew. "Poles can smell a Jew a mile away," my father said, "and sooner or later somebody will denounce us to the Germans." As a family, we could not pass ourselves off as Poles and expect to get away with it for long, and breaking up the family was out of the question. We continued our trek west to Kielce.

It seemed that we were condemned to be who we were, which was not a particularly good prospect. We could do little more than hope that things would get better. That hope never left us, and it sustained us in the years to come, despite the fact that we had no good reason to expect our situation to improve. But what else could we do but hope? That, after all, is human nature.

CHAPTER 3

The Ghetto of Kielce

WE LIVED IN KIELCE for about four years until we were transported to Auschwitz in early August of 1944. *Lived* is probably not the right word to describe our incarceration in that bleary Polish industrial city, its ghetto, and two different work camps. Had our train not been bombed in an area where Kielce was the nearest Polish city with a large Jewish population—it numbered about twenty-five thousand at the time—we would not have gone there; although, in retrospect, it made little difference that we did not reach another Polish city. The fate of Jews was basically the same in all of them, and life in Kielce during those years was no worse or better than it would have been elsewhere in Poland.

My first recollection of Kielce is our one-room apartment (kitchen included) on the third floor of an old, somewhat run-down apartment house on Silniczna Street. The building was part of a four-building complex that surrounded a dirty courtyard. To reach our house, one had to go through a big gate, which opened onto a noisy street. We were assigned the apartment by the Jewish community council of the city shortly before the ghetto was established in early 1940. At that time, the German police (the *Schutzpolizei*) and the Gestapo ordered all Jews to move into the area of the city containing the largest concentration of its Jewish population, which was also among the most run-down parts of the town. We did not have to move because we already lived there.

Until my father got a job as a cook's helper in the *Schutzpolizei* kitchen outside the ghetto, we had very little to eat. During those early days, food could still be bought from the outside. The more prosperous Jewish families lived relatively well compared to us, since we had hardly any money, even after my mother sold almost all her jewelry. In his new job, my father would return home every evening with a large canteen of food. He usually hid pieces of meat under the mashed potatoes and vegetables he was allowed to take with him. By midafternoon each day, my mother and I would already be waiting for him and our one good meal. From time to time, we were invited by wealthy families in the neighborhood to join them for a Sabbath meal. I remember looking forward to these dinners because of the food. But I also dreaded them because they were always preceded by what seemed to me to be interminably long prayers.

Soon, I too found a way to get some food and on rare occasions even a little money. Because religious Jews are not allowed to work on the Sabbath or on Jewish holidays, they may not perform most household chores on those days, including lighting ovens and fireplaces and turning on lights in their homes. These chores had in the past been performed by non-Jewish servants or Poles hired for that purpose. When these people were no longer allowed to enter the ghetto, I was asked by some of our neighbors, who knew that we were not observant Jews, to perform these functions. That is how I became a *Shabbat goy* (a Sabbath gentile). I liked doing these chores, not only because I was paid for them but also because in that way I got to know many families in the neighborhood and was able to see what their homes looked like and how they lived. I was fascinated by the appearance of the very orthodox Jews—their long *payess* (sideburn locks), their *tzitzit* (cloth fringes), their black hats and caftans, as well as the *talaysim* (prayer shawls) and the *tefillin* (phylacteries) they wore on their arms and foreheads when praying. But the majority of the people in the ghetto were not orthodox and dressed just as we did.

Once all Jews had been moved into what became the Ghetto of Kielce, the area was surrounded by walls and fences and guarded by Jewish and Polish police as well as the *Schutzpolizei*. There were many children in our neighborhood, and I soon had lots of friends. In those early days, some Poles were still allowed to come in, mostly to sell vegetables, milk, and firewood. When winter came, Polish farmers would enter the ghetto with their horse-drawn wagons to sell firewood, which was very expensive. We kids would wait for them and jump on the backs of the wagons, hoping that the drivers would not see us before we had a chance to grab some of the wood and run off with it. If a driver saw us, he would try to slash at us with his long whip. Sometimes he would succeed, despite the avoidance techniques we developed over time. Besides needing the wood, we had a lot of fun playing this game, particularly since our parents, while not approving of our wagon jumping, were always pleased to get the few pieces of wood we brought in.

Another game I remember playing with my friends was hiding in the empty field behind our apartment complex. There, from time to time, we could watch the Polish peasant women urinate in a standing position, with their legs spread out but without lifting their long skirts. At some point we would whistle or bang on a can in the hope of startling them and making them change their stance—with the predictable results. We would then run away laughing, while the women would hurl terrible Polish curses at us.

Once, two of my friends and I found a leather box of *tefillin* used by religious Jews in their prayers. Somebody had told us never to open such a box, that it was a sin to do so, and that God would strike down anyone who took out the little piece of parchment it contained, with its Hebrew inscription from the Torah. But we had also heard that if you found that piece of parchment and put it under your armpits, you would be able to fly. Well, we had quite a dilemma on our hands: we wanted to be able to fly but were afraid of God's wrath. Eventually, and with trembling hands, we cut open the box, expecting lightning to strike us right then and there, but nothing happened. At this point, one of the older boys very cautiously placed the parchment under his arm and readied himself for takeoff. Again nothing happened. Then, one after the other, we each tried the same maneuver. The result was the same. Disappointed but still afraid of God's punishment, we threw the box away and promised not to tell anyone what we had done.

In Poland, the expression *Yekke*, a somewhat derogatory term of ridicule, was applied by Polish Jews to German Jews who spoke no Yiddish or Polish and who, because of their appearance or demeanor, were thought by many Polish Jews to look more like gentiles and to be naive in matters of business. To Polish Jews, my mother was a *Yekkete* (a female *Yekke*), and when she and I walked down certain streets, we were frequently called *Yekkes* by the children in those neighborhoods. Once, while walking alone on one of the streets where I had previously been with my mother, I was surrounded by a group of boys my age and somewhat older. They began to push me around, made fun of my clothes, and kept calling me "*Yekke putz, Yekke putz*," the latter being a bad word I had been told never to use. I managed to run away but promised vengeance. My opportunity arrived soon, when a few days later I saw a boy walking with his mother on our street and recognized him as one of my tormentors. I raced up behind him, gave him a push with all my might, and ran away. He fell and cut his lip. When his mother saw the blood, she began to scream and wail, hurling vile Yiddish and Polish curses at me, my family, and my descendants. I could hear her from the far side of our courtyard where I was hiding. My mother was very mad at me when she heard what I had done, and told my father. I expected to receive a severe spanking, but after hearing the whole story, he said that it was good that I was learning to defend myself, and while he did not approve of my hitting the kid from the back, it was too late to do much about it.

Soon life in the ghetto became increasingly more difficult and dangerous, and our games began to give way to fear that kept us off the streets. There was one German—I no longer know whether he was from the Gestapo or the *Schutzpolizei*— who would come into the ghetto and randomly kill people as he walked down the street. He would walk up behind them, shoot them in the back of the neck, and move on. News that he had entered the ghetto would spread like wildfire, and in no time at all the streets would be deserted. I once saw him from a distance and ran home as fast as I could. After that, I was afraid to play in the street and no longer thought that our courtyard was safe.

As time went on, the Germans would, with ever greater frequency, conduct so-called *razzias*, or raids, in the ghetto. As a rule, these raids would begin with a contingent of heavily armed soldiers driving up to a house. They would storm inside, pull people out, and drag them into their trucks. Anyone who resisted was kicked and beaten. Some people were shot on the spot. Once, when I heard a lot of noise in our courtyard, I ran to the window and saw Germans pouring into the building across from us. Minutes later, I heard terrible screams coming from one of the apartments there. It served as a *chaydar* (religious school) as well as the living quarters of the rabbi, who taught a few children there in violation of the prohibition against teaching. The rabbi's wife and grown daughters were made to undress and stand naked in the courtyard while the rabbi, his hat knocked off his head, was dragged out of the house by his beard and taken away.

At other times, the Gestapo or the *Schutzpolizei* would drive into the ghetto, randomly grab men with beards, and order them to cut off each others' beards and sidelocks. Those who resisted were severely beaten. The soldiers seemed to be enjoying themselves. They would laugh a lot and make fun of their victims, who were shaking with fear and pleaded to be allowed to keep their beards. Jews also had to doff their hats when encountering a German soldier on the street. If a Jew did not do so, the Germans would knock his hat off and beat him. But if he did, they would frequently also beat him, yelling, "Why are you greeting me, you dirty Jew? I am not your friend!" My father solved this problem by never wearing a hat, not even on the coldest days of those terrible Polish winters. "Why give them the pleasure?" he would say when people called him a *Meshoogene* (crazy man) for not wearing a hat.

Every so often, we heard that this or that community leader or some other person had been picked up by the Gestapo, never to be seen again. My father and mother would discuss these events in whispered tones. Then I would hear one of them say that the victims must have been denounced to the Gestapo by our own people and that one had to be very careful what one said and to whom. "Yes, the walls have ears," one of them would invariably say, and while I did not quite understand what that expression meant, I soon learned not to tell anyone what I heard in our apartment or in those of our neighbors, where my father and mother and their friends would gather in the evenings to talk and share some vodka that someone had been able to find.

Not long after the ghetto was established, the Jewish community council put my father in charge of the office that allocated living quarters to the many people who had been moved into the ghetto. He did not really want that job since it put an end to the food he brought home from the police kitchen, but he felt that he could not refuse. The previous head of that office had been dismissed because of mismanagement and allegations of widespread corruption in the assignment of apartments. Not long after he took this job, my father threw two men out of our apartment. My father was very angry, and I later heard him tell my mother that the men had tried to bribe him with a lot of money to assign them a bigger apartment. That prompted my mother to ask why he did not get us a bigger apartment now that he had that power. My father just looked at her, shaking his head in disbelief; we continued to live in the same little place assigned to us when we first arrived in Kielce.

After bringing some order to the ghetto housing office, my father was put in charge of the *Werkstatt*, or workshop, which resembled a small factory. Here tailors, shoemakers, furriers, hatters, and other artisans had to work for the Gestapo and *Schutzpolizei*, performing whatever tasks they were ordered to do. For the most part, they made clothes and shoes for the officers and their wives. The *Werkstatt* was just outside the ghetto walls, which meant that my father and all those who labored there had permits to leave the ghetto to go to work.

Not long after my father became the head of the *Werkstatt*, my parents found out that my maternal grandparents had been deported from their home in Göttingen, Germany, to the Ghetto of Warsaw. How they got that news I do not know, but I remember my parents talking day and night about my grandparents and what could be done to bring them from Warsaw to Kielce. At some point I heard my father say, "I'll talk to one of the officers of the *Schutzpolizei*. His wife has a big appetite for the fur coats we have been making for her; he also seems to be more human than the others." Not long after, my grandparents arrived in our ghetto. To me it was a miracle, the nicest thing that had happened to us in years. My mother was very, very happy, and I finally had grandparents like some of my friends.

Thomas's grandmother, Rosa Blum-Silbergleit

My grandparents were provided with a room in a house not far from where we lived. I would visit them daily and hear wonderful stories about my mother when she was a young girl, about her brother, Eric, who lived in America, and about their life in Göttingen before the Nazis came. They had seen me a few times when I was just a baby, but as far as I was concerned, this was my first meeting with them. Visiting them was to enter another world, a world far removed from the ghetto, one full of love and tranquility. Here, I felt safe and protected. The stories they told me about the past and the future transported me into a world in which all people lived in peace and where being a Jew was not a crime.

The two families we were closest to in our apartment house were the Friedmanns and the Lachses. They were related to each other and still lived in their prewar apartments, one floor below us. My father and mother would often be guests in their homes, and I would play there with their children, Ucek and Zarenka, who were cousins. Zarenka was about four years old; Ucek must have been a year or so older. When I asked why the Friedmanns and the Lachses always had good food, I was told that they were rich and that when the war was over, we too would be rich again and have all the food we could eat. It was not easy for me to understand why we had to wait for the end of the war to be rich, but I kept these thoughts to myself.

One morning in August 1942, while it was still very dark, we were awakened by loud honking, repeated bursts of gunfire, and announcements over loudspeakers: "*Alle raus, alle raus! Wer nicht raus kommt wird erschossen!*" ("All out, all out!

Thomas's grandfather, Paul Silbergleit

Whoever does not come out will be shot!") The ghetto was being liquidated or, in the words bellowing out of the loudspeakers, *"Aussiedlung! Aussiedlung!"* ("Evacuation! Evacuation!") People were screaming and crying all around us. My mother immediately began to pack some of our belongings, while pleading with my father to hurry up. He was standing over our kitchen sink, shaving very deliberately and telling my mother to be quiet. "Let me think!" I heard him repeat over and over again. It was all very eerie, and the noise outside was getting louder and louder. When my father finished shaving, he put away his straight razor, helped my mother pack a few more things, and told us to follow him. There was shooting all around us, with one or two gunshots at a time coming from some of the houses the Germans had begun to search. When they encountered sick or old people who could not leave, they would simply shoot them on the spot and move on. We were the last family to come out of our building, just ahead of the marauding German death squads.

Our courtyard was crowded with our neighbors, who were trying to get away from the soldiers and their incessantly barking dogs that seemed to be trained to attack when their handlers yelled *"Jude!"* ("Jew!") My father pushed through the crowd, trying to lead us out of the courtyard with his *Werkstatt* pass in hand. Whenever he recognized one of his workers, he would urge them and their families to follow him. Gradually, some twenty to thirty people joined our group.

Along the way, we tried to find my grandparents, but they were nowhere to be found. I never saw them again. To this day, I can still see them—their smiles when I entered their little apartment—and the feeling of peace and happiness their embraces and kisses brought me.

As my father led us toward the ghetto wall and the entrance to the *Werkstatt*, we were stopped again and again by heavily armed soldiers, who would yell and point their guns at us in a most threatening manner. That was very scary. There was still a lot of shooting all around us. Dead people were lying in the streets, and we could not be sure that the German patrols we encountered would not shoot us as well. As soon as we were stopped, my father would inform the soldiers, in roughly the same tone of voice as they used when addressing us, that he was under strict orders by the commandant of the city to protect the *Werkstatt*. We would then be allowed to continue. "Never show them that you are afraid of them," I remember my father telling me time and again.

When we reached our destination, my father locked the gate and told everyone to settle down for the day. The shooting continued all around us for much of the afternoon. After a while, some men in our group pleaded with my father to let us march out "before they come in and kill us all for disobeying orders." He would have none of it and insisted repeatedly that our chances for survival were much greater if we remained in the *Werkstatt* until things had calmed down in the ghetto.

We stayed in the *Werkstatt* a few more hours. Had we wanted to, we could have escaped from there into the Polish part of the city, but without false papers and a lot of money we would soon have been caught and most likely executed. So we remained in the *Werkstatt* until the shooting had died down. At that point, my father decided that the time had come for us to move out. Once again, we were stopped repeatedly by German patrols. My father would inform them that he was under orders to bring the workers of the *Werkstatt* to the officer in charge of the evacuation. We would then be allowed to continue on our way to a large square.

Along the way, we passed a group of German soldiers. They had surrounded two young Poles who were on their knees, pleading for their lives. Next to them were two sacks with part of their contents strewn around. One of the Poles was wearing the whitest shoes I had ever seen. The soldiers were kicking the young men and yelling that looting was punishable by death. Then they shot them. For years afterward, whenever I saw or heard that someone had been shot, it would invariably revive memories of that terrible scene —the young man on his knees, and those white shoes.

As we approached the square, we could see a group of Gestapo and *Schutzpolizei* officers facing a large crowd of ghetto inmates, all pleading to be allowed to cross over to the other side of the yard, where the people were standing who had been selected to remain in Kielce after the liquidation of the ghetto. As we entered the yard with my father in the lead, the commandant of the *Schutzpolizei*, who was a frequent customer at the *Werkstatt*, recognized my father. "We need him," he exclaimed, "he runs the *Werkstatt!*" and he motioned my father to the other side. My mother, holding on to me, followed. When a soldier tried to stop us, the officer motioned him to let us through. Once we were together, my father pointed to the group he had led out of the *Werkstatt* and told an officer that they were his workers. They too were allowed to join us.

From a distance I could see Ucek and Zarenka, my little neighbor friends, standing in the square with their parents and the other people who were to be sent away. A short time later, as we were moving out of the courtyard, Mrs. Friedmann somehow managed to push Ucek and Zarenka toward my mother, their "aunt Gerda," pleading with her to "save them, please save them!" The children ran over to us. My parents immediately moved toward the middle of our group in order to hide Ucek and Zerenka among the grown-ups. The two children cried silently as we left the square. My mother sought to console them by whispering that they would soon see their parents again. That was not to be, for all those who were forced to remain in that square and the others who had been evacuated earlier in the day, including my grandparents, were transported to Treblinka and killed on arrival in that extermination camp. In all, more than twenty thousand people—almost the entire Jewish community of Kielce— were massacred in that operation.

Those of us who were not sent to Treblinka when the ghetto was liquidated ended up in an *Arbeitslager*, or labor camp. It occupied a small area of the former ghetto. The two or three streets that composed this area abutted a field that at one time may have been a large playground or park. When we got there, it was just an empty, dusty plot of land. Our family, with Ucek and Zarenka now part of it, was housed in a large room, with a kitchen and bathroom that we had to share with another family. The bathroom had a big tub in which we three children got a chance to be bathed from time to time. Here I was very happy because I now had a brother and a sister, and, besides, I was the big brother and could lord it over them.

We arrived at the labor camp in the late fall of 1942 — I was eight at the time — and remained there for about a year. My father still ran the *Werkstatt*, while my mother struggled to feed the five of us on the meager rations we got, which was not easy. Except for the fact that our family had grown and that Ucek and Zarenka were my constant companions, only two events from our life in the labor camp stand out in my mind.

Once, my mother received an order from the commandant of either the Gestapo or the *Schutzpolizei* (I don't recall which it was), summoning her to present herself to him the next day. She spent the remainder of the day in a terribly worried state, crying much of the time. When my father heard of the summons on his return that evening, he turned pale, and while he told her not to worry, I could see that he too was very concerned. They kept wondering all evening why the commandant would want to see my mother and what would happen to her. "Do you think that it has something to do with the children?" she asked. "That's not it," my father assured her. "They would simply have come and dragged the children away." More speculation followed, and then my father said that he had figured it out and that they would talk about it later. At that point, I started to cry because I thought that the Germans planned to kill my mother.

At night, I heard my father and mother continue to whisper about the order she had received. My father explained that he was sure that the Germans wanted her to become an informer. There could be no other reason for this strange summons, he claimed. If they had wanted to punish her for something, they would simply have come for her, and that would have been the end of it. No, he was sure that they wanted to use her as an informer because, among other things, she spoke German, and they could communicate directly with her. The problem was, my father explained, that if they told her what they wanted her to do and she refused, they would kill her or send her to Auschwitz or some other concentration camp. And if she did as they asked, she would eventually suffer the same fate. What to do? My father saw only one way out: "Don't let them tell you what they want you to do. Just keep changing the subject. Talk about Göttingen, about anything, but for heaven's sake, don't let them tell you that they want you to work for them."

The next day, my mother was picked up and taken to the office of the commandant. I thought I would never see her again, and when Ucek and Zarenka saw me crying, they also cried and kept asking when Mutti was coming back. She did return and seemed no longer worried. When my father arrived that evening, she greeted him with a big smile and a kiss. "You were right," she said, "but I never let him get to the point. He must think that I am a babbling idiot and that I was too dumb to be of any use to them."

The other event that has stayed with me to this day was the liquidation of the labor camp. It began early one morning. The Germans drove into the camp, ordered everybody out into the street, and herded us toward the big field in the middle of the camp. There we had to line up in two long columns, a dozen people abreast. The two columns were separated by a passageway some five meters wide. When we had been properly lined up, the soldiers (I believe both the *Schutzpolizei* and Gestapo participated in this operation) began to walk up and down between the two columns looking for children. The entire operation was overseen by the German city commandant. He stood in front, at a distance of about ten meters, facing the two columns. From time to time, he would bark out some order to his subordinates or flick his riding boots with a short horsewhip.

All around us, children were being torn from the arms of their parents. When the soldiers saw Zarenka and Ucek, they tried to wrest them away from my mother. The two children began to scream, and my mother tried to hold on to them, but one of the soldiers began to beat her and she had to let go. Then one of the soldiers saw me and tried to drag me out as well. Holding on to me, my father stepped into the passageway. As the soldier was getting ready to beat him as well, my father bellowed something, and the man stopped. Still holding me by the hand, my father walked up to the city commandant. Before my father could say anything, I looked up at the commandant and said (I don't know why or whether it was at my father's prompting), *"Herr Hauptmann, ich kann arbeiten"* — "Captain, I can work." He looked at me for a brief moment and said, *"Na, das werden wir bald sehen"* — "Well, that we'll soon get to see." Then he motioned my father and me back toward the column where we had been standing.

We learned later that Ucek and Zarenka, with about thirty other children, were first locked up in a nearby house. From there, in the late afternoon, they were taken to the Jewish cemetery, where they were killed. We heard afterward that the soldiers used hand grenades to murder them. In that cemetery in Kielce there stands a monument today, erected in memory of the children who were killed on that terrible day in 1943, among them my little brother and sister. That is what they had become and that is what they will always be as long as I live. Over the years, I have managed to erase from my memory many a horrendous thing I experienced in the camps, but never for a moment have I been able to forget the day when Ucek and Zarenka were taken from us.

What prompted the city commandant to spare my life on that morning has remained a mystery to me. Was it that I was blond and spoke fluent German and possibly reminded him of his own children? I shall never know.

After the liquidation of the labor camp, we were divided into two groups of a few hundred people each and sent to two different factory complexes on the outskirts of Kielce. One group went to Ludwików, a large foundry. My parents and I ended up with the other group in Henryków, a large saw-mill that manufactured wooden wagons for the German war effort. The iron rims for the wheels of the wagons made in Henryków were produced in Ludwików. In Henryków, we lived in a big barrack with all the other workers. My mother, father, and I slept in bunks toward the back end of the barrack, separated from our neighbors by a thin curtain. I do not remember whether the *Werkstatt* was still in existence and whether my father still ran it, but I think it more likely that he now worked full-time at some machine in the factory. My mother served as a nurse in the small infirmary presided over by Dr. Leon Reitter, the only doctor not executed when all the Jewish doctors who survived the liquidation of the ghetto were killed in the labor camp a few months before the children were murdered.

Soon I too had a job. My parents were afraid that the German officer who had let me live because I told him I could work might one day come to Henryków on an inspection tour and ask about me. Since I had not been assigned a job in the factory, my parents decided that I should try to get the German head of Henryków, a civilian manager by the name of Fuss, to hire me as his errand boy. In order to speak to Fuss, I waited for him one day outside the small house where he had his office, and I approached him as he came out. When I told him what I wanted and that I also spoke Polish, he looked me up and down, and just when I was sure that he was not going to hire me, he said that he could use me. That's how I became his errand boy.

My job consisted mainly of taking the mail to a special mailbox, running various errands for Fuss on the factory grounds, and parking the bicycles of the Germans who visited him. It did not take me long to figure out that these Germans were noncommissioned officers who did not qualify for the cars the higher Gestapo and *Schutzpolizei* officers came in. I feared the latter and tried to avoid them as much as possible. The ones on bikes seemed less threatening, although I knew from experience that any German in uniform was to be avoided. Whenever these men would arrive at the building that housed Fuss's office, I had to take their bicycles and place them in the bike rack some twenty to thirty meters away. At first, I pushed the bikes obediently to the bike rack. Gradually, I began to ride them like a scooter, with one foot on a pedal. As time went on and I became surer of myself, I would try to ride the bikes. I was much too short to sit on the saddle and could barely reach the pedals. Besides, never having learned to ride a bike before, I fell off a few times. While I did not mind a few scratches here and there on my hands and knees, I was afraid that I might damage the bikes and get into serious trouble. These were sturdy military bikes and could withstand considerable rough treatment, but had their owners or Fuss caught me trying to ride them, I would certainly have been severely punished. That never happened, and I eventually learned to ride a bicycle. Later, when teaching my sons to ride a bike, I often wondered whether they realized that there were more perilous ways of learning the art than to have a father hold on to the saddle until he thought that it was safe to let go.

Fuss was in the habit of walking through the factory halls and yards with a whip. When he saw prisoners who were not working, he would beat them severely with his whip. He administered these beatings indiscriminately to men and women alike, frequently hurting his victims quite badly. After seeing one such beating, I decided to try to alert the workers that Fuss was on his way. As soon as I saw that Fuss was getting ready to make one of his rounds, and if I did not have other chores to perform for him, I would run ahead of him through the factory halls. Since Fuss usually wore a Bavarian hat with a feather, I would signal his imminent arrival by wiggling my finger at the top of my head. I got a big kick out of performing this service and probably saved many a prisoner from a beating.

In the evenings, I would tell my mother and father what I had been doing that day as Fuss's errand boy. On one occasion, I mentioned that I could hear the radio broadcasts Fuss listened to in his office. He usually had the radio on quite loud, and when I sat in the corridor near his door, I had no trouble hearing everything being said. Once I even heard Hitler speak; I was sure that it was Hitler because the person sounded just like my father when he put on a Hitler imitation for our closest friends. That was a very dangerous thing to do, and my mother always warned him that someone might denounce him to the Gestapo, but my father seemed to relish doing it. My report about the radio broadcasts prompted my father to suggest that I listen very carefully, try to memorize as much as possible what I heard, and report to him in the evening all I could remember. That became my regular assignment. Thereafter, whenever I had a chance, I would listen to Fuss's radio and sometimes also to what he and his visitors were talking about. One day, I thought I heard that Mussolini had been captured by partisans. Since I knew that Mussolini was Hitler's friend, I could barely wait to tell my father all about it. For a while, no one wanted to believe me, but then the news was confirmed by some Polish workers who were regular employees at Henryków. From then on, my reports on what was being broadcast on German radio were eagerly awaited. But our joy over Mussolini's capture was short-lived, for we soon learned that he had been rescued by the Germans.

The perimeter of the Henryków factory was guarded by soldiers who were, we were told, Tatars. They must have gone over from the Soviet side to the Germans when taken prisoner and were serving in German auxiliary units. They were not heavily armed, which apparently prompted some young men in our barrack to believe that it would be easier to escape when the Tatars were on duty. One night, some of these prisoners cut through the barbed wire fence. The Tatars, who always struck us as less committed to guard duty than their German counterparts, nevertheless spotted the attempted breakout. They shot and killed one of the escaping prisoners on the spot and captured the others. We were, of course, awakened by all the shooting and screaming. The next morning, the Tatars turned the prisoners over to the Gestapo, who drove away with them. Some days later, after gallows had been erected in front of our barrack, the prisoners, badly beaten and barely able to walk, were brought out. We had to line up and watch the hangings. The prisoners were ordered to stand on chairs under the gallows while the Germans forced an equal number of inmates, standing on ladders, to pull the nooses over the hoodless heads of the condemned prisoners. I could see that the hands of one of the inmates were shaking violently as he struggled to put the rope over the prisoner's head. The prisoner turned and kissed the man's hand, said something to him, and slid his head through the noose. The Gestapo officer in charge of the execution saw what had happened and furiously kicked the chair out from under the prisoner. It was obvious to us that the valor of the condemned man had robbed the German officer of much of the pleasure he must have expected to derive from his death. As I watched this horribly tragic scene, I was gripped by a curiously perverse sense of Schadenfreude, for it was only on very rare occasions that we could claim to spoil the pleasure the Gestapo appeared to derive from tormenting us, and this was one such occasion.

The bodies of the prisoners were left hanging for a few days near the entrance to the barrack as a warning against further escape attempts. There were to be other executions in Henryków. As time went on, they became routine; but I remember only the first. The dignity and humanity the young prisoner demonstrated moments before his death—and the disdainful refusal of the other condemned men to plead for their lives—no doubt served over time to reinforce my conviction that moral resistance in the face of evil is no less courageous than physical resistance, a point that has unfortunately been frequently lost in the debate over the lack of greater Jewish resistance during the Holocaust.

Our life at Henryków came to an end abruptly one morning in July 1944, almost a year after we got there. A large contingent of German soldiers entered Henryków and ordered all of us to line up in front of the barrack. Then we were marched under heavy guard to what I believe was the freight railroad station of Kielce. When we got there, we found that the prisoners who had ended up in Ludwików when the labor camp was liquidated were already at the station. Here a freight train was waiting for us, and we were all ordered to get in. The doors were then locked from the outside. There was little light in the cars, although we could look out between the slats on either side. I saw that the last car of the train was an open cattle car bristling with heavy machine guns pointing in all directions. Soldiers with submachine guns sat in little cabs above each car.

As we were boarding the train, we heard various announcements over the loudspeaker. One informed us that our next destination would be a factory in Germany where we were needed. This announcement was greeted with considerable relief and for a while seemed to silence the whispered rumors that we were on our way to Auschwitz. While I could not quite imagine what Auschwitz was really like, I had heard terrible stories about it, and I could sense that the mere mention of the name sent shivers down the backs of my parents and the other grown-ups.

Many hours passed as the train moved through the Polish countryside. Asked where he thought we were being taken, my father assured everybody in our car that the train appeared to be moving toward Germany, not Auschwitz. Having studied at the university in Kraków, not far from Auschwitz, my father knew that part of the country well. Sometime later, I heard my father whisper to my mother that the train had veered off the route to Germany and was moving in the direction of

Auschwitz. Others soon realized what was happening. People began to cry and pray; others huddled together in whispered conversations. I remember my father taking a big gulp from a small bottle of vodka before passing it to my mother. My mother kept squeezing my hand and hugging me from time to time.

Two men in our car started to pry open some floorboards in the middle of the car. Similar escape plans were apparently being hatched in other cars. As it got dark and while the train was traveling near a forested area, machine-gun fire, coming from the last car, exploded all around us. Our guards must have spotted those who were trying to escape by sliding through the holes in the floor of the cars and lying very flat between the rails. We never found out whether any of these prisoners made it. The train did not stop, and the shooting continued for some time. There appeared to be some additional escape attempts, followed by more gunfire, but the rest of us resigned ourselves to the fact that we would soon be arriving in Auschwitz.

CHAPTER 4

Auschwitz

I WAS TEN YEARS OLD on that sunny morning in the first days of August 1944 when our train approached the outskirts of the concentration camp of Auschwitz. Actually, as we were to find out later, we were on our way to Birkenau, located some three or four kilometers down the road from Auschwitz proper. It was in Birkenau that the gas chambers and crematoriums had been erected, and it was here that millions of human beings died. Auschwitz proper was merely the public front for the Birkenau extermination camp. Auschwitz was shown to visiting dignitaries, whereas Birkenau was the last place on earth many of the prisoners sent there were destined to see.

As the train moved closer and closer to Birkenau, we could see hundreds of people in striped prison uniforms digging ditches, carrying bricks, pushing heavy carts, or marching in formation in different directions. *"Menschen!"* ("Human beings!"), I heard someone mutter, and I sensed a collective sigh of relief in our car. "After all, they do not kill everybody on arrival," must have been the thought that flashed through our minds. The mood in the car lightened somewhat, and people began to talk again. "Maybe Auschwitz is not as bad as it has been made out to be," somebody said. I thought that it looked just like Henryków, only bigger, and that it would not be all that bad.

Years later, when asked about Auschwitz and what it was like, I would reply that I was lucky to get into Auschwitz. This response would invariably produce a shocked look on the face of the person who had asked the question. But I really meant what I said. Most people who arrived at the Birkenau rail platform had to undergo a so-called selection. Here the children, the elderly, and the invalids were separated from the rest of the people in their transport and taken directly to the gas chambers. Our group was spared the selection process. The SS officers in charge must not have ordered it because they probably assumed, since our transport came from a labor camp, that children and others not able to work had already been eliminated in those camps. Had there been a selection, I would have been killed before ever making it into the camp. That is what I meant with my flippant remark about being lucky to get into Auschwitz.

Of course, when we arrived in Birkenau, I did not know what to expect, nor did I know that I had escaped the deadly selection process. As soon as we stepped out of our freight cars onto the station platform, all men were ordered to line up on one side and all women on the other. But for one brief moment a few months later, this was the last time I was to see my mother until we were reunited on December 29, 1946, almost two and half years after our separation. We could not really say good-bye, because the SS guards were constantly yelling for us to move, hitting and kicking anyone who did not immediately do what they were ordered to do. I was too scared to cry or even to wave to her and stayed close to my father.

My father held on to me as we were marched away from the station toward a big building. Here we were ordered to take off our clothes and made to run through some showers and a disinfecting foot pool. Along the way, our hair was shorn off, and we were thrown the same blue and white striped prison uniforms we had seen on entering Auschwitz. It was at this point that my father whispered to me that we had made it, for it was only when we had received the uniforms that he could be sure that we were not being taken to the gas chambers.

With that process behind us, we were again ordered to line up and march. We must have walked for quite some time before we came upon rows and rows of barracks as far as the eye could see. Streets—actually unpaved roads—cut through the long rows of barracks. High barbed wire fences on either side of the rows of barracks divided what looked like a large town into sizable individual camps, each with its own gate and guard towers. Later I was to learn that these individual camps were identified by letters of the alphabet. For example, women were housed in camps B and C, men in camp D, and so on. Our destination was camp E, better known as the Gypsy camp. That camp had housed many thousands of Gypsy families. All of them—men, women, and children—were murdered shortly before we arrived. Only the name remained to remind us of yet another horrendous crime committed in the name of the master race.

The entrance to the Gypsy camp, consisting of a movable barbed wire gate, was guarded by the SS with their dogs. Once inside the camp, we were ordered to line up in single file behind a group of barracks and made to roll up our left sleeves. At one end of the line, two inmates sat at a wooden table. Each of us had to move up to the table, state our name, and stretch out our left arm. I was walking ahead of my father in the line and did not quite know what was happening. Then I saw that each inmate at the table was holding something that looked like a pen with a thin needle at the end, and that they were writing something on the outstretched arms after dunking the pens into an ink pot: we were being tattooed. When my turn came, I was afraid that it would hurt, but it went so fast that I could hardly feel it. Now I had a new name: B-2930, and it was the only "name" that mattered here. The number, now somewhat faded, is still there on my left arm. It remains a part of me and serves as a reminder, not so much of my past, but of the obligation I deem incumbent on me, as a witness and survivor of Auschwitz, to fight the ideologies of hate and of racial and religious superiority that have for centuries caused so much suffering to mankind.

My father, who was right behind me in the tattoo line, became B-2931. Our numbers were also printed on a strip of cloth with a yellow triangle, the color identifying us as Jews. (There were different colors to distinguish between different types of inmates. Political prisoners, for example, were given red triangles. Other colors were assigned to homosexuals, criminals, and so on.) Some forty-five years later, when I returned to Auschwitz and gave the person in charge of the archives my name in order to find out when precisely I had arrived there in 1944, she asked for my number. I looked surprised since I had always heard that the Germans kept very precise records in their camps. "By the time you arrived," she explained, "there was such a large influx of new arrivals that the SS no longer bothered to record the names of inmates, only their numbers." Sure enough, once she had my number, she was able to provide the date I needed. The card with my number even disclosed how many people had come with me to Auschwitz from Kielce. It occurred to me then that unlike those of us who survived Auschwitz and can document our existence in that camp by reference to our numbers, those prisoners who died in its crematoriums after the SS had stopped recording their names have left behind no trace of their presence in that terrible place. No bodies, no names; only ashes and numbers. It is hard to imagine a greater affront to human dignity.

After we had been tattooed, we were assigned to our barracks. Ours was a wooden structure like all the others in the Gypsy camp, with a mud floor that divided two long rows of wide, triple-level, wooden bunks. Once in the barrack, we were greeted by a burly prisoner with a cane. This, I was to learn right away, was the *Blockältester*, or barrack boss. He kept pointing to the bunks and yelling in Polish and Yiddish, "Ten men to each level!" Whoever did not move fast enough for him was hit or kicked. My father and I found a bunk, picked the middle level, and were soon joined by eight other inmates. Then we were ordered to lie on our stomachs with our heads pointing toward the middle of the barrack. I can't recall whether we were given blankets, but I am sure that we had no mattresses.

Although we were not given anything to eat that evening, the very thought of food was forced out of my mind by what happened that night. Into the barrack strutted two or three well-fed inmates with canes and clubs. They wore armbands that identified them as *Kapo*. Kapos were inmates who, together with the barrack bosses, ran the camp for the SS and terrorized their fellow inmates, day in and day out. Right after the Kapos had greeted our barrack boss, one of them yelled in German, "Spiegel, you son of a bitch. Get down. We want to talk to you!" As soon as Spiegel stood before them, the men surrounded him and started to hit him with their fists and clubs: on his face, his head, his legs, his arms. The more Spiegel begged for mercy and screamed, the more the Kapos beat him. From what I could make out as the Kapos yelled while beating him, Spiegel had apparently denounced one of them to the Gestapo in Kielce, with the result that the denounced man had been sent to Auschwitz some two years earlier.

Spiegel was soon on his knees and then flat on the ground, begging to be allowed to die. He was covered with blood and no longer really trying to protect himself against the blows that continued to rain down on him. The Kapos then picked up Spiegel and began to push and pull him out of the barrack. We did not see what happened next. Later we heard that the Kapos had dragged Spiegel to the fence and that he died on the fence. Our camp, like the others in Birkenau, was enclosed by a highly electrified fence that emitted a perennial buzz. The fence separated those of us in the Gypsy camp from camp D on one side and camp F on the other. A single wire strung about a meter high and a meter from the fence on either side warned inmates not to get any closer lest they be electrocuted. Spiegel must have died by being thrown against the fence or by crawling into it. Gradually, I came to realize that it was not uncommon for inmates to commit suicide by what was known as "walking into the fence."

It is difficult not to wonder whether it ever occurred to these Kapos that they were no different from Spiegel. He denounced fellow Jews to the Gestapo because he believed that he was thereby prolonging his own life, whereas the Kapos allowed themselves to become the surrogates of the SS by beating their fellow inmates, forcing them to work to total exhaustion, and depriving them of their rations, knowing full well that by these actions they hastened the deaths of the prisoners. All that in order to improve the Kapos' own chances of survival. Thus, besides testing the morality of those who became neither informers nor Kapos, the concentration camps were laboratories for the survival of the brutish. Both Spiegel and the Kapo he had denounced had been friends of my parents. Both had been with us in Katowice. At that time they had been my "uncles." I seem to recall that the Kapo whom Spiegel had denounced had been a dental technician or a dentist in his prior life; I never knew what Spiegel's profession had been. Had they not ended up in the camps, they probably would have remained decent human beings. What is it in the human character that gives some individuals the moral strength not to sacrifice their decency and dignity, regardless of the costs to themselves, whereas others become murderously ruthless in the hope of ensuring their own survival?

I remember very little about my activities in the days immediately following the Spiegel beating. Of course, I thought a lot about my mother and missed her very much. I wondered what she was doing, whether they had also cut off her hair as they had ours, whether she had enough to eat, and whether she had to live in a barrack similar to ours. In those early days, I was also introduced to the Auschwitz feeding system. We would be awakened early in the morning and made to line up in front of a big kettle from which an inmate with a ladle would pour out a liquid that looked like black coffee. Next to him stood the barrack boss, cutting slices of black bread. The bread was frequently moldy and the slices rather small. I soon noticed that not everyone got the same amount of bread. Those the barrack boss did not like would get a smaller piece or no bread at all, while his friends and he himself would keep whole loaves. Complaints would invite a beating. In the evening, we would be served the day's only other meal. It consisted, as a rule, of some tasteless, watery turnip soup. Since we got no bread in the evening, I would try to save a little piece of my morning bread for later in the day, hiding it very carefully so that it would not be stolen.

That, more or less, was all we had to eat. On such a diet, some people gradually became *Muselmans*, the name given to inmates who had become totally emaciated, walked around in a stupor, stopped eating altogether, and in no time died quietly. I soon learned that if somebody became a *Muselman*, he would not live very long. That was the fate of a friend of my parents whom I had called "Uncle" for as long as I could remember. He and his wife had been with us in Katowice. He was Jewish; she was not. And while, as a German gentile, she could have left him and gone back to Germany, she refused to do so and helped him as best she could. In Kielce, she lived outside the ghetto and somehow managed to get food to him; she did the same in the labor camp. I still remember them talking over the fence in the ghetto. Access to Auschwitz or anywhere near the camp was closed to her, and he, a big man, simply could not live on the rations we received. When I saw him a few weeks after we had arrived in Auschwitz, he was the skinniest human being I had ever seen. He no longer recognized my father or me and kept mumbling to himself. After the war, my mother and I visited his wife, who had returned to her native Hamburg. Of course, she wanted to know when I had last seen her husband and whether I knew what had happened to him. I lied and told her that the last time I had seen him, he was his usual friendly self, although somewhat thinner. I simply could not bring myself to tell this woman, whom we all admired for her courage and loyalty to her husband, the truth about his last days. She had suffered enough.

I do not remember how long my father and I remained in the barrack we occupied when we first arrived in the Gypsy camp. A Kapo who took part in the terrible beating of Spiegel was in charge of a barrack that served as a kind of warehouse, where the clothing taken from people on their arrival in Auschwitz was sorted and eventually shipped out. Where it went, I never knew. To help us, the Kapo had my father and me and a few of his other friends from Kielce assigned to his barrack. We slept there and worked there. In many ways, this was a lifesaving break for us. We were no longer subjected to the maltreatment dished out in the other barrack, we had a little more food, and we had a bunk bed with blankets and a straw mattress. Equally important, we could keep warm with some of the clothes stored in the barrack.

In our new barrack, my father and I shared a bunk with my friend Walter and his stepfather. Walter had managed to avoid being murdered with the children of Kielce because he was a few years older than most of them and was rather tall. After we had moved into our new barrack, Walter got very sick. His father took him to the infirmary, where he was admitted after being diagnosed with diphtheria. The barracks serving as the infirmary of the Gypsy camp were located kitty-corner across from our barrack. Less than a week after Walter had entered the infirmary, we were awakened one night by terrible noises coming from across the street. SS trucks with their motors running were standing outside the infirmary, while SS guards herded screaming patients into the trucks. Of course, the patients knew that they were being taken to the gas chambers, and we knew that the SS was thinning out the population of the infirmary to make room for new patients. They would do that every few weeks; that is why it was so dangerous to go to the infirmary. In the morning, we learned that Walter was among those who had been taken away. His stepfather kept blaming himself for Walter's death because he had taken him to the infirmary, but we all knew that he had had no choice, given Walter's illness. I still do not understand how it was possible for Walter to come down with diphtheria while I, sleeping next to him, escaped being infected. Was it just luck, or is it possible that he did not really have this highly contagious disease?

Every few weeks, the SS would enter the Gypsy camp and embark on its periodic selections. These selections were usually conducted by one or two SS doctors, most often under the supervision of the infamous Dr. Mengele, known as the Angel of Death, whose very name made me tremble with fear. The selections would take place early in the morning, after all the inmates had been lined up in front of their barracks and counted. Even when there was no selection, the daily counting process was an ordeal that could take hours, particularly when someone appeared to be missing. The missing person usually turned out to be an inmate who had died overnight. The daily counting was frequently accompanied by beatings and at times also by hangings. Soon after we had arrived in Auschwitz, my father, seeing how routine selections were conducted and that children were most at risk, came up with a strategy to beat the system. Every morning when we had to line up for the daily counting exercise, I would try to stand all the way in the back and very close to the entrance of the barrack. As soon as we had been counted and if it appeared that there might be a selection, I would try to slip back into the barrack and hide. That strategy saved me a number of times. It was not always easy to execute, however, because I had to disappear without being seen by the SS or the barrack boss, but I was never caught.

Selections were sometimes also conducted randomly.

Mengele would enter the camp with some of his assistants and order any children or sick or old people he encountered in the barracks or walking outside to be taken away. My father discussed this problem with our Kapo friend, who suggested that a real job might provide me with some protection. A few days later, I was hired by the Kapo of the sauna, as the camp's bathhouse was called. Here newly arrived inmates from other subcamps were given a walk-through shower and had their clothes disinfected. My job—I now think that it may have been created as a favor to my father's friend—consisted mainly of running errands for my new boss. Whenever an SS guard stopped me somewhere in the camp, which happened from time to time, I would identify myself as the sauna's errand boy and be permitted to be on my way. The job gave me a greater sense of security than I had had before when meeting up with an SS guard, although it was always hard not to tremble when called over by one of them.

At times too I would have to deliver a message or a package to someone at another camp. I try in vain to recall how I was able to leave and come back, but I remember being sent once, together with another person, to one of the crematoriums (we used that term generically to refer both to the gas chambers and the crematoriums). We had to pick up the gas my sauna boss needed for the disinfection of clothes. Of course, I was terribly afraid to go near the place but had to do it anyway. When we got there, we were greeted by inmates who worked at the crematoriums. Their job was to remove the bodies from the gas chambers and burn them in the crematoriums. They were all strong young men who joked around with us, probably because they sensed that we were terrified to be so close to the gas chambers. After we told them what we had come for, they gave us some containers of gas to take back to the sauna. The person who had accompanied me thought that we had been given the same Zyklon gas that was used to kill people in the gas chambers. I have no way of knowing whether that was true, although it made some sense, considering that we got it from the crematorium.

The air in Auschwitz always smelled foul because of the smoke that came out of the crematorium chimneys. The odor and smoke was strongest with every new transport that arrived in Birkenau, because the people who could not pass the initial selection process on the station platform were immediately herded into the gas chambers. Whenever the crematoriums were being operated at night, the sky above them would take on a reddish brown color. One summer, many decades after the war, I visited Auschwitz and saw birds and wildflowers in what used to be Birkenau. It suddenly struck me that I had never seen a bird before in Auschwitz. The smoke must have kept them away. Nor can I remember seeing any grass or trees there. The soil turned to mud when it rained and remained mud for days on end, except in the winter when a mixture of dirty snow and ice covered the ground.

There was one barrack in the Gypsy camp where we could wash. Its water, always a rusty brown color and always ice cold, came streaming out from small holes drilled in the long pipes that hung above sinks that resembled feeding troughs for cattle. Another barrack served as a communal toilet. There, holes cut into long rows of elevated concrete slabs served as toilet seats. This was our favorite camp location because it was the only place where it was always warm. But we were never allowed to stay there longer than a few minutes. This rule was strictly enforced by an inmate caretaker from Greece. I will never forget him. He played the mandolin very beautifully when not chasing us out. I soon learned that if I told him that I loved his music, he would let me stay a little longer in that warm toilet.

One day, it may well have been in late October, we were awakened for what appeared to be a selection, although it differed from the previous ones I was familiar with. We had no idea what was happening, since the SS was not following its routine selection procedures. Instead of being counted as usual on such occasions, we were lined up, barrack by barrack, and herded into a barrack toward one end of the camp. Once inside, we had to move in single file past a group of doctors who stood facing us at the end of the barrack. I believe Mengele was there, but I cannot be sure since I never really dared to look. SS guards were posted a few meters apart throughout the entire length of the barrack and on either side of the panel of doctors. My father walked in first, and I followed behind him, looking for an escape route. There was none. When we were just a few meters away from the doctors, one of them motioned my father to the left and me to the right. My father tried to pull me with him, but an SS guard grabbed me while another kicked my father out of the barrack. That was the last time I saw my father.

I was taken to an adjacent barrack. It was guarded by an inmate who must have been the barrack boss. When I arrived in that room, some other people were already there. Most of them looked sick; others were old, and some had become *Muselmans* or were close to it. There was another entrance at the end of the room. That door was kept closed with a piece of wire. Seeing my opportunity, I stationed myself close to the door and waited. More people were brought into our room, all no different from those already there. They seemed resigned to their fate. I was not! I knew that our destination was the gas chamber and that I had to find a way to escape in order to rejoin my father. Moving ever closer to the door and keeping my eye on the barrack boss, I began to unwind the wire. It came apart rather easily, and I bolted out of the door. Behind me, I could hear some fellow inmates yell that I was escaping. Alerted, the barrack boss raced out and caught me. He slapped me around a few times and dragged me back to the barrack. I managed to get out of the room twice more but was caught each time and hit again.

At that point, I decided that I would not be able to escape and that in a few hours I would die in the gas chamber. At first, I was terribly angry with my fellow inmates who had given me away each time I had tried to escape. I could not understand why they had done that. My escape would certainly not have affected their fate, and they must have known that they were on their way to the gas chamber. Then I thought of my father and how upset he must be because, unlike in the past, he had not been able to keep me from getting caught in a selection. I would like to have been able to tell him that he should not blame himself, for he could not possibly have anticipated the trap we had walked into.

With these thoughts still swirling in my head, I moved to a corner of the room, away from the door, and sat down. After a few minutes, I realized that I could no longer hear any voices around me, nor the barked orders of the SS guards in the nearby barrack. Until then, I had been gripped with fear, fear of dying, for I realized that, having failed to escape, I was on my way to the gas chamber. But then something most unusual happened. Slowly, very slowly, my fear and anxiety faded away as I admitted to myself that there was no way out and that I would die in a few hours. The nervous tension that had hung over me like a cloud lifted. An inner warmth streamed through my body. I was at peace, my fear had vanished, and I was no longer afraid of dying.

When the selection had ended, there were some thirty to forty inmates in our room. We sat there waiting for the truck that would take us to the gas chamber. Nothing happened for a while, and then an SS truck rolled up, and we were ordered inside. At first, the truck moved in the general direction of the crematoriums, but then it veered off slightly and entered the nearby *Krankenlager*, or hospital camp, which I believe was camp F. The camp consisted of a number of barracks that housed prisoners who were sick or quarantined. The truck rolled up to one of these barracks, and we were ordered out. Here we were received by orderlies who took down our numbers on small index cards and made some other notations on each of them. Pressed to tell us why we had been brought to them, we were told that we were there "in transit." The SS had apparently concluded that it would be a waste of resources to take our small group to the gas chamber, which would also have meant starting up one of the crematoriums. They decided instead to keep us in this camp until they had put together a larger group.

The barrack in which we were housed held inmates with a skin disease: scabies, or *Krätze*, in German. They appeared to have scabs all over their bodies and scratched all the time. Every morning they would line up, be inspected by a young Polish doctor, and usually be given an orange salve. I was afraid that I would catch this disease and went to see the doctor a few times. He was always very kind to me and gave me advice on how to avoid coming down with scabies. On one occasion, he handed me a piece of soap—it had been quite a while since I had seen soap—and told me to wash my hands frequently. Every so often, he would examine me and express delight that I had not contracted scabies. He made sure that I always had enough soap. From time to time, he also slipped me some bread and arranged for me to be moved to a corner bunk at the other end of the barrack, away from the entrance and those parts of the barrack where the other inmates tended to congregate.

When I was pretty sure that I would be able to avoid getting scabies, I began to like my life in the hospital camp. *Maybe the SS forgot us*, I thought, hoping that I was right, and for a while, it seemed that that is what had happened. The only unpleasant part about being in that barrack was its proximity to the crematoriums. Many a night I would wake up to screams and pleas for help coming from the crematorium area, as people were being herded into the gas chambers. It was terrible. At first I would lie awake shaking. Then, when I fell asleep, I would have nightmares, terribly scary and vivid nightmares in which I was being beaten or executed. They made me afraid to sleep because the same nightmares kept returning night after night. After a while, without realizing what was happening, I had found a way to cope with my nightmares: In my sleep, while the nightmare was upon me, I would hear myself say, "This is only a nightmare; there is nothing to be afraid of." And the nightmare would vanish. After that, whenever I was half awakened by the horrified screams coming from the nearby gas chambers, my mind would unconsciously transform them into nightmares, and I would continue to sleep.

Then, one night, when I kept hearing terrified voices all around me, I went right on sleeping, believing that I was again having one of my nightmares. But when I woke up the next morning, I was told that the SS had come during the night or very early in the morning and dragged out all the people who had been brought to this barrack with me. It was a miracle, I thought, that the SS had not found me. Soon, though, I learned how I had been saved. When we first arrived at this barrack, a red X had been placed on the backs of our individual index cards. My friend, the young Polish doctor, apparently tore up my card and issued me a new one without the red X. When the SS came in and demanded the cards with the red mark, my card was not among them. The doctor had saved my life, and my nightmares saved me from witnessing what was happening that night and possibly giving myself away.

I remained in the hospital camp for another week or two. Then one day the doctor called me to his little cubicle and told me that I was to be moved to the children's barrack in camp D. Having learned to be suspicious—not of him, of course, but of the people with whom he had arranged my transfer—I kept asking him how he could be sure that my destination was camp D and not the gas chamber. He assured me that I had nothing to worry about. That turned out to be true. A few hours later, I was taken to the children's barrack in camp D. To this day, I don't really know how this transfer was arranged. All I remember is that I was picked up by an SS guard, the oldest SS guard I had ever seen. He did not look like the other SS guards I had encountered. They were usually young, seemed to pride themselves on their military bearing, and appeared to enjoy mistreating us. This man was kind and kept telling me that I would like the children's barrack in D camp and that I would be safe there. He was the first SS guard in whose presence I did not fear for my life. Later, I heard that by 1944 old men were being drafted into the SS because the young ones were needed at the front. It may well be that this SS guard was one of these draftees.

Before I arrived in the children's barrack, I did not know that such a barrack existed. I was told later that it was the brainchild of a German political prisoner. He had saved a group of teenagers from the gas chambers by convincing the SS that it made no sense to get rid of the kids when they could be made to perform useful work in the camp. The SS agreed to let him prove it and put him in charge of a barrack that housed only children. In time, other boys ended up in that barrack. Most, if not all, of the kids in the children's barrack were older than I. As soon as I had met the head of the barrack and was assigned to a bunk, I recognized two friends: Michael and Janek. I knew them from Kielce. They had survived the murder of the children in the labor camp of Kielce by hiding in the attic of the house where the children were being held before they were taken to the cemetery. I was delighted to see them again. Given our common Kielce experience, we became inseparable and thought of ourselves as brothers.

Garbage collection was the main job to which most of the children were assigned. Sometimes we also had to collect garbage in other camps. We would pick up the garbage in various places, put it in wooden carts, and take it to a garbage dump. Three or four kids were usually assigned to a cart. Michael and Janek somehow managed to have me put on their team. In general, our work was not very difficult. But when it rained, which happened often, our shoes and the wheels of our cart would sink into the mud, making pushing the cart much harder.

Once, we ended up close to one of the women's camps. We were sent to pick up some garbage in C camp, which was bordered on one side by our D camp, enabling the men and women in these camps to engage in yelling conversations across the electrified fence. My father had found out that my mother was in B camp, which meant that we could not see her from our camp. But as soon as we had entered C camp, Michael, Janek, and I, together with two other kids, began to push our cart close to the side of the fence that bordered B camp. Whenever we saw any women on the other side, we yelled over to them in Polish and Yiddish that they

should alert women from Kielce. A few minutes later, we recognized some women we knew from Kielce, among them relatives of Janek and Michael. Then I saw my mother. When
she saw me, she began to cry and call, "Tommy, Tommy!"
And if some women had not held her back, she would have
tried to touch me through the electrified fence. All I could
think of was that she was alive, while she kept repeating,
"Du lebst, du lebst!" ("You're alive! You're alive!") Then she
asked about my father. As I began to tell her that my father
had been shipped out on a transport, a woman Kapo raced
over and chased all the women away from the fence. For
months afterward, I kept replaying her words in my mind
and seeing her tear-covered, smiling face through the fence.
What mattered was that she was still alive and not a *Muselman:*
she was thin but looked well under the circumstances, and,
I kept saying to myself, she was very beautiful even without
her hair. Not long after that encounter, I heard that a large
number of women, including my mother, had been sent to
another camp in Germany.

Our barrack boss treated us well and distributed the rations
fairly. Only rarely did the rations suffice to overcome that linger-
ing feeling of hunger that had become part of me. Still, I always
resisted eating anything we found in the garbage. Since we were
also responsible for the garbage of the SS kitchen, the tempta-
tion was great to eat the remains of a sandwich or to lick a can
that still contained a few slivers of food or some drops of soup
or sauce. Whenever I saw such items in the garbage, I would
remember my father's repeated warning never to eat anything
from the garbage lest I get terribly sick. Once, though, a special

opportunity presented itself. While collecting garbage outside the SS kitchen, we looked through the open window and saw that no one was in the kitchen at that moment. Near the stove stood a pan filled with milk. It had been years since Michael, Janek, and I had tasted milk. We looked at each other, and without saying a word, Michael climbed into the kitchen through the window. He took a big gulp of milk, then passed the pan through the window to us. Janek and I took a few sips from the pan and handed it back to Michael. He put whatever was left of the milk back where he had found it and climbed out again as fast as he could. Had we been caught, our punishment would have been a very severe beating or worse. But we were not caught, and to this day I can still taste that heavenly mouthful of milk. No milk has ever tasted as good. Years later, when my own children would have to be coaxed to drink their milk, I would think of that milk in the SS kitchen and be grateful that they never had to risk their lives to get it. At the same time, I would have to hide my anger that they did not appreciate what it meant to have milk in abundance. But how could they? For many of us who survived the camps, food took on an almost mystical quality. Despite the fact that I am not religious, I consider it a sin to throw bread away, however stale it might have become, and will walk miles to feed it to birds or, remembering my job as *Shabbat goy* in Kielce, let my wife throw it away instead.

Not long after I had seen my mother, the older boys in our barrack reported in conspiratorial tones that there were rumors that the Germans were losing the war and that the Russians were approaching. I did not really know what to believe or what it all meant. The thought that we might soon be liberated never quite entered my consciousness. I could think only of the cold Polish winter that was upon us and the fact that it was ever more difficult to stay warm. It must have been late December 1944 or early January 1945. The soil under our feet was frozen. The mud was no longer a problem, but the ice made it hard for us not to slide while pushing the garbage carts. Of course, the garbage was also frozen and difficult to load. As we worked on breaking it up, we consoled ourselves with the thought that frozen garbage did not smell.

Then, one morning, we were awakened by repeated announcements coming at us in those harsh German command tones to which I never quite got accustomed: *"Das Lager wird geräumt!"* ("The camp is being evacuated!") We were ordered to line up in front of the barrack with our blankets and other possessions. My possessions consisted of a thin blanket, a spoon, and a metal container that served both as my cup and soup plate. I always had the cup tied by a string to the piece of rope that served as my belt. Next, we were ordered to march through the main Birkenau gate. The road outside the gate was already lined with thousands of inmates, standing about eight or ten people abreast. "Children to the front of the column!" came the order. Our barrack was to be in the lead. The column was so long that it took us quite some time to get to the front. It was freezing, and a very strong wind was blowing through our clothes. As we stood there waiting, we were thrown a loaf of black bread. Then the order came: *"Vorwärts marsch!"* ("Forward march!")

The Auschwitz Death Transport had begun.

CHAPTER 5

The Auschwitz Death Transport

AS WE BEGAN TO MARCH, leaving Birkenau gradually behind us, I looked back toward the vast stretch of land with its hundreds of barracks, administration buildings, guard towers, and electrified wire fences. Further in the distance, I could see the remains of the crematoriums that the SS had tried to demolish. I could not really believe that I was leaving this terrible place alive. I remembered what my father once said in the Ghetto of Kielce as he and a few friends shared a bottle of vodka: "Do not despair. Sooner or later we will win this war and bury them deep under the ground." And I could hear my mother trying to shush him by warning that "the walls have ears." But he would not be silenced. Years later, I wondered whether my father really believed what he had said, or whether it was vodka-induced optimism or hope or both. Now, as I looked back on this vast murder factory, I felt victorious and kept repeating to myself, as if addressing Hitler directly, "See, you tried to kill me, but I am still alive!"

Of course, the march had only just begun, and I had no idea what lay ahead. And what lay ahead turned out to be worse than anything I could have imagined. The roads were covered with snow and ice. It was January, after all, and a typical Polish winter. As the sun gradually set, it became colder and colder. The trees along some of the roads gave us temporary protection against the icy wind that would blow against us and pass right through our thin clothes. I was wearing my mother's boots, which she had given me before we reached Auschwitz. My socks had been taken away when I had arrived at the camp. In their place, I used some rags to keep my feet warm. Michael, Janek, and I stayed close together, trying to keep warm. We were getting tired and realized that those of us from the children's barrack, having been ordered by the SS guards to the front of the column of marchers, had it harder than those who followed on the snow and ice we had already trampled down. By late afternoon, Janek, Michael, and I found it increasingly difficult to keep up and decided to let the marchers pass us until the rear of the column was almost upon us. Then we jogged to the front again. Once we realized that this maneuver worked, we kept repeating it. Of course, we were getting pushed aside or bumped by the marchers, but that was a small price to pay for the respite it gave us.

It was already dark when the SS halted the march for the night and allowed us to sleep on the road where we had stopped and in the drainage ditches on either side. By that time, some marchers had already died. Those who could not go on and sat down by the side of the road or simply collapsed were shot by the SS guards, who kicked their bodies into a nearby ditch. Over the next two days, many more would die in this manner. After a while, I would no longer jump when yet another shot was fired. As I got ever more tired, and the cold, windy air began to hurt, I wondered whether it would not be easier to lie down and let them kill me. The prospect had its attraction because it would be speedy and liberating. But I would almost immediately banish that thought and push myself even more. "If I give up, they will have won," I kept muttering to myself. Staying alive had become a game I played against Hitler, the SS, and the Nazi killing machine.

After marching for three days, we reached Gliwice (Gleiwitz), a town some seventy kilometers from Birkenau. These three days have become blurred in my mind, making it difficult for me to identify the specific day on which a given event occurred. For example, I can no longer say with any degree of certainty whether it was toward the end of the first day or the second day that the SS decided that the children's barrack was slowing down the march. But I remember very clearly that it was just beginning to get dark when the SS halted the march and ordered the group from the children's barrack to the side of the road, to be taken "to rest in a nearby convent." At that moment, Michael, Janek, and I were not in front with our other friends from our barrack. Instead, we were once again doing our rest-and-jog routine and had come to a stop near the middle of the column. Despite the orders of the SS for children to come forward, we decided to stay where we were. Some men around us tried to push us out, but we fought them off. The three of us had learned long ago not to trust the SS. "Rest in a convent" sounded too good to be true. I was told later that our friends from the children's barrack had all been murdered. I do not know whether that is true, but I never saw any of them again.

A group of Russian prisoners of war was marching in formation in one part of the column. I had not seen them when we were leaving Auschwitz and thought that they might have joined our transport at some later stop. They attracted my attention because it was never easy to get around them when Michael, Janek, and I moved from one end of the column to the other. We were afraid of the Russians because we thought they kept jostling us in order to grab our bread. We held on to it as tightly as we could whenever we came close to them.

One evening the column was halted, and we were all ordered to sit down on the road. Everybody but the Russians obeyed the order. They remained standing and began to sing what must have been a patriotic song. An SS guard blew a whistle, and more than a dozen SS guards materialized out of nowhere and moved toward the Russians. *"Alle hinlegen!"* ("All down!") the SS officer in charge shouted. The Russians remained standing. Then the officer shouted something, and the SS guards opened fire. They must have killed some of the Russians, for a number of them went down. The shooting continued until the survivors sat down. I no longer know, if I ever did, what prompted this tragic episode. What I do remember, though, is that the standoff gave me an opportunity to rest and that I dozed off at some point, with the shooting and the screaming still ringing in my ears.

The next morning, after we had spent what I think was the second night sleeping on the road, I noticed that more people had died overnight and that others were too weak to continue. At that point, what was happening around me had become routine: the SS would kill those who refused to continue and order some nearby marchers to push the dead into the closest ditch. Increasingly, I blocked these scenes from my consciousness and no longer registered what was happening around me. I seemed to be in a trance as I struggled to walk in order to stay alive.

In the mornings, as soon as Michael, Janek, and I were fully awake, we would encourage each other to jump around and to rub our numb limbs. When I told them that I thought I could not feel my toes, Janek told me to wiggle them. I did, but that did not seem to help all that much. The cold was getting unbearable. We ate our remaining bread and licked a few handfuls of snow. That was our breakfast. Oh, what would I have given for even a few spoonfuls of that terrible Auschwitz turnip soup or, for that matter, anything warm!

We reached Gliwice, a Silesian industrial center, on the last day of our march and entered what appeared to be an empty labor camp. I began to fantasize that heated barracks, beds with blankets, and even warm food awaited us. But I was almost immediately torn out of this dreamworld when we came to a stop at the edge of a run-down sports field. A group of SS officers stood in the middle of the field, which was ringed by a large number of heavily armed SS guards and their dogs. It did not take me long to realize that another selection awaited us: those among us who could jog to the other side of the field would live; the rest would be eliminated. By this time, I could barely walk. Michael and Janek were not doing all that much better. We were exhausted, hungry, and cold, but we wanted to live, and we were not going to give up now after all we had been through on the march. As we looked out over the field, we could see people trying to make it across; some appeared to collapse along the way or simply just sat down. Every so often the guards would run over and drag these unfortunate people to the side of the field. When our turn came, we held hands to support each other and ran as fast as we could, which was not very fast. Dirty, with clothes torn, we must have looked like beggar children emerging from a dark cellar. We could hear the SS officers laugh hilariously as the three of us passed. These hated voices invigorated us and gave us the strength we did not have just minutes before, and we made it across.

We must have stayed in Gliwice for a number of days. Here we were able to rest and recover some of our strength. The food was no better than what we were given in Auschwitz, but at least we got some warm soup, and the bread portions seemed somewhat larger. Just as I was beginning to believe that we would remain in Gliwice, we were ordered to march out of the camp and proceed to a nearby railroad station. Here open rail cars, like those used for transporting coal or sand, awaited us. We were herded into these cars with so many other prisoners that there was hardly any room to move. Michael, Janek, and I found ourselves being pressed against the taller grown-ups and could barely breathe. Above us, at one end of the car, sat a heavily armed SS guard in what looked like a brakeman's cabin. Since the cars had no roof, the SS guard could see what was happening in the car and anticipate any escape attempts. I seem to remember that, before leaving, we were each given a loaf of black bread and a tin can that was supposed to contain meat. I never did find out what was in it since we had no can opener, knife, or even rock that would help us open it.

Our car was so crowded at first that, despite the fact that we were riding in open cars in January, Michael, Janek, and I were kept warm by the bodies that pressed against us. After a day or two, to avoid being trampled, we were able to work ourselves toward a corner of the car. People were dying all around us, and when our guard was asked what to do with the bodies, he said to throw them out. That was being done with increasing frequency as the days went by. Our car was gradually becoming less crowded until it was no longer difficult to walk from one end to the other. The snow and wind seemed never to let up, and we could feel the cold more now than before because there were fewer warm bodies pressing against us. Our bread was long gone, and all we had to eat was snow. We imagined that it was ice cream, although I doubt that we remembered what ice cream tasted like.

The nights in the car were horrendous. The hunger and cold were wearing people down not only physically but also mentally. Some began to hallucinate. They walked into the walls of the car, making noises like wild animals. They seemed to be seeing ghosts and monsters. They would fall over us or run into us and scream while waving their arms wildly as if trying to hit us. We soon noticed that these men seldom survived the night.

Just when I was sure that it would only be a matter of a day or two before I too would die and be thrown out of the car, a miracle occurred. As the train moved slowly through Czechoslovakia, making frequent stops, we began to see men, women, and children standing on the bridges we passed under. They waved to us and shouted, and then loaves of bread began to fall into our train. Under the first bridges, Michael was able to catch a loaf and told me to hold on to it while he and Janek readied themselves for the next bridge. I put the bread under my legs. When they came back, the bread was gone. Somebody had managed to steal it out from under me, and I was too numb to feel it. But we soon had more bread because the Czechs kept throwing it at us from the bridges. Had it not been for that Czech bread, we would not have survived. I never learned how this magnificent campaign had been mounted, but as long as I live, I will not forget these angels — to me they seemed to be angels — who provided us bread as if from heaven.

We were fortunate that the train could not take the shorter and more direct route from Gliwice to Germany, our final destination. By the end of January 1945, the Allies had severely damaged the German rail system, forcing our train to take the route through Czechoslovakia. That proved to be our salvation. Of course, had the train been able to proceed directly to Germany, some of those prisoners who died while we were traveling through Czechoslovakia might have survived.

Our train reached Germany after a trip that lasted more than ten days. The one stop in Germany that I remember most vividly was a freight station in Berlin. Here, I believe, we remained for only a few hours before going on to Oranienburg, some forty kilometers away, where the concentration camp of Sachsenhausen, our final destination, was located. I had two experiences at that station in Berlin that I have never forgotten. Shortly after the train had come to a stop, I heard a German woman exclaim for all to hear, *"Es stinkt schon wieder von Juden!"* ("It stinks again of Jews!") About an hour later, our new SS guard—they changed guards every few days—climbed off the train and got himself a cup of coffee. He must have seen me looking longingly at his cup. Without a word, he handed me the coffee and got himself another cup. This was my first warm drink since we left Gliwice.

Beyond being able to attribute the German woman's outburst to a deep-seated hatred of Jews and acknowledging the action of the SS guard as an unexpected act of compassion, I have never been able to reconcile these two events to my own satisfaction, other than to end up with the trite conclusion that generalizations about the Holocaust, about German guilt, or about what Germans knew or did not know do not help us understand the forces that produced one of the world's greatest tragedies. Nor do they help explain what it is in our nature that enables human beings to plan and commit the genocides and the many other mass murders to which mankind has been subjected during my lifetime. Of course, even less do they answer the question of why, in the midst of all these terrible events, some people find the strength and moral courage to oppose or, at the very least, not commit these monstrous crimes that others perpetrate with ease.

We arrived in Oranienburg not long after leaving Berlin. Instead of going directly to Sachsenhausen, we ended up at the Heinkel airplane factory. We spent about two weeks there, supposedly in quarantine—at least that is what we were told. Here Michael, Janek, and I, together with others from our transport, were housed in a large hangar. The hangar was warm, and even though we slept on the ground, it was a relief finally to be inside with a roof over our heads. My feet had already begun to hurt on the train. But because of the cold and snow, I had been afraid to take off my shoes there. Now in the hangar, I removed my shoes for the first time since leaving Auschwitz and noticed that my feet were swollen and discolored. But I did not let that worry me since I convinced myself that after a few days in a warm place everything would be fine again.

Our rather comfortable life at the Heinkel factory came to an end sooner than I would have liked. One morning, we were ordered to proceed on foot to Sachsenhausen. Michael and Janek were with me, together with other men from our Auschwitz transport. It was becoming increasingly more difficult for me to walk, but my two friends helped me along. In order to get from Heinkel to Sachsenhausen, which was not all that far, we had to walk through Oranienburg. Here the German townspeople stared at us or turned their backs as we passed. Along the way, some children threw stones at us. I was relieved when I finally saw the entrance to the concentration camp of Sachsenhausen with its inscription: *Arbeit macht frei*. (Work makes you free.)

This slogan, so utterly bizarre given its context, was no more bizarre than the policies that brought us to Sachsenhausen. In January 1945, Germany was fighting for its survival, and yet the Nazi regime was willing to use its rapidly dwindling resources — rail facilities, fuel, and troops — to move half-starved and dying prisoners from Poland to Germany. Was it to keep us from falling into the hands of the Allies or to maintain Germany's slave-labor supply? The lunacy of it all is hard to fathom, unless one thinks of it as a game concocted by the inmates of an asylum for the criminally insane.

CHAPTER 6

Liberation

THE BARRACKS IN SACHSENHAUSEN WERE ARRANGED in a semicircle along the periphery of the *Appellplatz* (exercise grounds)—all within range of the machine guns mounted on the balcony of the SS administration building and the guard towers along the camp's wall. From the *Appellplatz*, one could see slogans painted in big white letters over the dirty walls of the barracks proclaiming, *Reden ist Silber; Schweigen ist Gold* (Talk is silver; silence is gold), *Arbeit macht frei* (Work sets you free), and *Freiheit durch Arbeit* (Freedom through work). In the middle of the *Appellplatz* stood a structure that resembled a village well. It was the camp gong or bell. Every morning, it summoned the inmates to the *Appellplatz* where they were to be counted. The roll call meant hours and hours of waiting for the counting to end.

For those of us in the *Revier* (infirmary), where I ended up not long after arriving in Sachsenhausen, the gong did not mean standing in line for hours. Here the orderly would simply call out our names, and if there was no answer, he would walk over to the bed from which he expected a reply, glance quickly at the person lying there, cross out the name, and continue counting. This short interruption in the counting process rarely produced any expressions of grief on the part of the other patients. It had become routine, a nonevent.

As soon as I arrived in Sachsenhausen, I was forced to accept that my feet were severely frostbitten. I had tried for a week or more to avoid going to the infirmary, although the toes on my right foot were getting blacker by the day. Those on the left foot were also rather discolored but not as badly as the toes on the right foot. I was afraid to go to the infirmary because I knew from past experience in Auschwitz that the surest way to end up in the gas chambers was to enter the sick ward of a camp. But my pain kept getting worse, and Michael and Janek—we stayed together after we arrived in Sachsenhausen—kept telling me that I had nothing to lose by having a doctor look at my toes. They finally convinced me and helped me get to the infirmary. On the way, I kept telling them that all I needed was some cream or other medication, and my feet would be fine. I was certainly not going to stay in the hospital and let them kill me after they cured me, which was as likely to happen in Sachsenhausen as it had been in Auschwitz.

When I arrived at the hospital, I was told to take off my shoes. A person in a white coat, who seemed to be in charge, took a quick look at my feet and told me to lie down on a big wooden table. Then he stepped out of the room and soon returned with some other men. Before I knew what was happening, two of them appeared on either side of the table.

As if on command, they grabbed my arms and legs and held me down. I started to scream, but a white towel or gauze was placed over my face, and I could feel a fluid with a very strong odor being poured over the gauze—it was ether, I learned later. I was out almost immediately. When I woke up, I was in a hospital ward in a single bed. As soon as I realized that the lower parts of both my legs were heavily bandaged, I got terribly scared. "They amputated my feet!" I sobbed. That, I knew, meant death once the SS guards embarked on their next regular hospital selection, looking for the sickest inmates to kill.

I asked one of the orderlies what had been done to me, and he said that two of my toes had been amputated. I did not believe him and decided to see for myself. Although at that point I really did not feel anything because the anesthesia had not yet worn off entirely, I started to complain of terrible pain. I continued to cry until a doctor came. After asking me some questions, he began to take off my bandages. That really hurt, but I was not going to stop him: I had to know whether I still had my feet. When I saw that my feet had not been amputated, and even though I could not really make out how many of my toes were gone, I relaxed, totally exhausted and in even more pain.

Although the doctors had amputated only two of my toes, the others on both feet had also been frostbitten, though much less severely. Over the next few weeks, they worked very hard to save the remaining toes. In the meantime, I was slowly recovering from the operation. At first I walked on crutches but soon managed to move about with the aid of a

cane or a single crutch. I considered that quite an achievement because I had been terribly worried that I would never
walk again. Now I began to believe that the doctors and
nurses were telling the truth when they assured me that my
toes would grow back. "After all," they would say, "don't you
remember that when you were little, your teeth fell out and
you got new ones?" "Yes," I replied, "that is true." "It's the
same with toes — if they are cut off only once before you are
twenty-one, they will grow back, just like your teeth."

Not long after my operation, a man who had been visiting
another patient stopped by my bed. He wanted to know my
name, where I had been before I ended up in the infirmary,
and whether my foot still hurt. He told me that he came from
Norway, that his name was Odd Nansen, and that one of his
friends, also from Norway, was in a nearby bunk in my ward.
Mr. Nansen returned a few days later with cookies, a picture
book with big letters, and a pencil. "You need to learn to read
and write and to draw pictures," he said. Thereafter, whenever he came to visit, he brought me something to eat, usually
sweets, which I had not seen or tasted in years, and he always
wanted to know what progress I had made with my writing. I
later learned that the Norwegian and Danish inmates of the
camp received food packages from the Swedish Red Cross,
which they frequently shared with other inmates. Every so
often, Mr. Nansen would also speak with the ward's orderly,
hand him something (usually tobacco or cigarettes), and tell
him to take good care of me. Soon I came to look forward
to Mr. Nansen's visits, not only because he always brought
me something nice, but also because we talked about many

things, especially about what we would do once the war was over. He sounded very much like my father when he kept saying that the Germans would soon lose the war, that I would then go to school with other children, learn to read and write, and be reunited with my parents. Mr. Nansen also spoke frequently of his wife and children in Norway. He expected to see them as soon as we were liberated and promised that I would get a chance to meet them.

The barrack that housed my ward in the infirmary was constructed of wood, like most of the other barracks in the camp. It had a few little windows and one or two round ventilation holes cut out of the ceiling. I had never noticed these holes. They had always been closed until they were forced open one day. Not long after I had arrived in the infirmary, I realized that more and more Allied airplanes were flying over the camp at night as well as during the day. They were on their way to bomb Berlin. After a while, as the flights overhead increased and more bombs fell on Oranienburg, the Allies began to drop flares around the camp's perimeter to ensure that our camp would be spared. The sound of the bombing was terrifying and made our barrack shake, but we felt safe, knowing that they were trying to protect us. Then one day, as the planes were again flying over, there was a tremendous explosion that shook our barrack more violently than usual, followed by an even louder scream from one of the beds. "They hit me, they killed me, the bastards!" I heard a man scream. Everyone who could sit up did. Then we all burst out laughing as if on command. One of the covers of the ventilation holes had been forced loose by the explosion and had fallen on the man. When he realized that it was not a bomb and that he was still alive, even he could not resist laughing. I don't remember ever laughing before, either in Auschwitz or Sachsenhausen. This was the first such occasion, and it brought us some welcome relief, although, given where we were, there was something macabre about the laughter resounding around the room.

Our SS guards gradually realized that the camp was the only place that could provide a safe haven from Allied bombing raids. Soon we heard that many of them would bring their families into the camp whenever the air-raid sirens sounded in Oranienburg. Oh, how we relished this information, and how it must have irked them. To think that the Germans now finally feared for their lives and had to seek protection in our camp! That made us feel good, even though one or two stray bombs did fall just inside the camp wall and killed a few inmates.

At regular intervals, a loudspeaker in our ward broadcast Nazi propaganda news. We had developed a special system for listening to it. For example, whenever they reported that five German fighter planes had shot down thirty Allied bombers and their fighter escorts, we assumed the opposite to be true. News from the Western or Eastern front was treated by us in the same way. Then, one day, a special news item caught our attention: "The Jew Roosevelt, President of America, has died!" the announcer gleefully repeated a number of times. Of course, we assumed that Hitler had died and started to congratulate each other. This time, unfortunately, it was not Hitler but Roosevelt who had in fact died.

I don't remember whether it was before or after the news of President Roosevelt's death that Mr. Nansen came to see me as usual. This time he looked very troubled as he told me that he and the other Norwegians would be leaving the camp within the next few days to be taken to safety in Sweden. He said that he had tried everything to be allowed to take me along, but it was unfortunately not possible. In any event, we would all be free soon and meet again after the war. He gave me a strong handshake, wrote down his name and address on a piece of paper, and told me to take good care of myself. I was very sad after he left and wondered whether I would ever see Mr. Nansen again. Much later I realized that Mr. Nansen had probably saved my life by periodically bribing the orderly in charge of our barrack with cigarettes and tobacco to keep my name off the list of "terminally ill" patients, which the SS guards demanded every few weeks "to make room for other inmates."

Not long after Mr. Nansen left, I woke up one morning to the usual sound of the camp gong. The sun was not shining, and it promised to be a rainy day. I remembered that the bandages on my foot would have to be changed again. This was always very painful because too much skin had been cut off around the amputated big toe, leaving an exposed bone over which the doctor, every few days, tried to pull the skin. The thought occurred to me that it would be wonderful if I woke up one morning and found that my toes had begun to grow again or, at least, if I could find some excuse for not having the wound rebandaged. At that point, the orderly came into the room without his usual list. Rushing through the ward, he announced that Sachsenhausen was being evacuated. Everybody able to walk had to get up and line up on the *Appellplatz*.

The barrack was suddenly very quiet. The silence was interrupted only by the closing of the door as the orderly left the ward. There were people with me in this big drab room whose legs had been amputated, and others who were in body casts. Others still were in the final throes of some terrible disease. Certainly none of these individuals could leave. I decided that I could make it and started to get dressed. So did a few others in the room. They must have been thinking what I was thinking, and that made all of us hurry. Camp evacuation meant long marches and overcrowded trains, like those that had brought me to Sachsenhausen. But it also meant that people who could not walk would be shot wherever they were found—on the roadside or in their beds. I imagined seeing the SS guards with their big boots walking from bed to bed in the infirmary, shooting everyone left behind.

I found my cane and a piece of bread and limped out of the room, leaving behind the moans of those who could not get out of their beds. In the small hospital yard, separated from the other barracks by a wire fence, people were hurrying toward the gate leading to the *Appellplatz*. As I followed them, I suddenly realized how fast I was walking. My foot did not seem to hurt. I only hoped that the SS would not notice me with my cane. I knew that I had to be evacuated with the camp's other inmates if I wanted to stay alive.

When I reached the *Appellplatz*, I started to look for Janek and Michael. They were nowhere to be seen. I wondered whether they had been shipped to another camp, for they had visited me only once shortly after my operation. Hundreds of people were standing around on the *Appellplatz* with blankets over their shoulders and pots or canteens in their hands. The SS guards were in full combat dress. They appeared nervous, and the dogs that were their constant companions barked much of the time. I managed to walk unnoticed to a spot near the rear of a column. Now a long wait began. Many hours passed. Rain started to fall, making standing difficult. I ate the piece of bread I had saved from the day before. The nerves on my right foot began to twitch, giving me the sensation that the amputated toes were still there. I could feel them wiggle and pressed my left shoe on my right to stop it. That did not really help much. I was very tired and finally sat down.

After what seemed a long, long wait, the first column started to move out through the main gate under the administration building. At that point, I noticed a group of five men with blankets and rucksacks on their backs. They stood close to where I was sitting. One of them was a doctor I knew from the hospital who had always been very kind to me. I limped over to him, and he greeted me with a smile. "Doctor, may I march with you?" I asked. "Yes, of course," he said, looking at my cane and the oversized shoes I was wearing, given to me in the hospital. "We are going to try to leave with the second transport tomorrow morning. Half of the camp is leaving today and the others tomorrow. You should go back to the hospital and get a good rest." "But, doctor, are you also going back to the hospital?" I asked. "I don't want to stay behind." He assured me that he was and told me to join him and his friends as they walked back to the infirmary. On the way, the doctor asked me whether my foot hurt. I lied and told him that it did not. I was afraid to tell him the truth because I feared that he would not want to take me along if he thought that I could not make it.

During our walk back, the doctor and his friends reported that the front was getting closer, that the Soviet troops were nearing Sachsenhausen and Berlin, and that we would soon be liberated. I had heard similar talk before the evacuation of Auschwitz. People said that you could hear the sound of artillery from the approaching front if you put your ear to the ground and that the war would soon be over. That was in January 1945, and now it was already April, and I was in yet another camp. That explains why I was not particularly excited about all this talk of our impending liberation. Besides, I could never quite believe that there would actually come a time when the war would be over and I would be free and able to go to school. Once, when Mr. Nansen told me that after the war I would learn to read and write in a school with many other children, I remember wondering whether school would be like a big concentration camp for children, but where there would be lots of food and I would never be hungry again.

When we had reached the infirmary, the doctor told me to go to my ward and get a good night's sleep. As I opened the door of my ward, I could sense fear gripping the patients who had stayed behind. They must have expected the SS with their dogs and guns. There was a general sigh of relief when they recognized me. I was swamped with questions and reported what I had heard: that the Russians were coming closer, that there would be another transport tomorrow, and that there was nothing to worry about tonight. Then I went to sleep with my clothes and shoes on in order to be ready the next morning.

The sun was shining through the small windows of our ward when I woke up. I jumped out of bed as fast as I could and hurried over to the ward where the doctor had his quarters. The door was open but nobody was inside. Everything pointed to a sudden departure. There were empty cans, paper, and rags on the floor and on the straw mattresses of the beds. As I hobbled through the room, I called out the name of the doctor. There was no answer. Fear choked my throat as I realized what had happened. "The doctor left me behind!" I cried. I limped out of the room into the hospital yard and through the gate. The *Appellplatz* was totally deserted! But I remembered the machine guns on the balcony of the administration building and on the guardhouses. Without looking up at them, I limped back to the barrack as fast as I could, trying to stay close to the wall in order not to be seen by the SS guards behind those guns.

"He left me behind!" I cried, throwing myself on the floor next to the bed of Marek, my Polish neighbor whose legs were in a cast. Marek must have been in his midtwenties. Except for me, he was the youngest person in the ward. We had become friends as soon as he had arrived at my ward. "Why didn't you tell me? Why didn't you wake me up? I don't want to die with you. I don't want to die!" He pulled me up to his bed and, with tears in his eyes, told me that the last group had left either late at night or early in the morning. I don't know how long I had been sitting on his bed when I heard him whisper, as if talking to himself, "They were going to take my casts off next week. Now they'll bury me with them." I limped over to my bed. My feet hurt. Moans and muffled cries filled the room. *This is it*, I thought.

A little while later, I heard Marek say, "You can walk. Why don't you leave the hospital and hide someplace in an empty barrack?" This possibility had not occurred to me, not even when I realized that the doctor and his friends had deserted me. Had I thought of it, I probably would have tried to hide. Now, as I lay in my bed with my clothes on and the cane by my side, I did not want to hide anymore. I had lost the desire to live and the fear of dying. It was a wonderful feeling, complete emptiness. My feet seemed no longer to hurt; I was not hungry anymore. *I hope they come soon*, I thought, as I remembered having had a similar sensation in Auschwitz when, with no hope of escape, I waited for the truck that was to take me to the gas chamber.

Hours passed, and I realized that I was still alive. The pounding of heavy artillery made our barrack tremble. Some people were sitting up in their beds looking at their neighbors, as if to reassure themselves that they were still alive. In between the heavy bombardment, we could hear machine-gun fire. "They must be fighting in Oranienburg already. Somebody should go and see what is happening." Marek turned to me. "You can walk," he said. I slid down from the bed, limped out of the ward, and began to crawl along the outer wall of the barracks through the hospital yard to the gate.

The *Appellplatz* was deserted. Not far away from me something fell to the ground. It looked like a piece of metal. Heavy machine-gun fire could be heard coming from different places outside the camp's wall. I looked up at the balcony of the administration building. There was nobody behind the big gun. I walked a few steps further until I could see another watchtower along the wall of the camp. It too was empty. I limped back to the ward as fast as I could, stormed through the door, and screamed, "They are gone, they are gone! The SS has run away! The machine-gun towers are empty!"

Very excited, I reported what I had seen. Nobody seemed to believe me because Marek called me over to his bed and asked whether I might have been mistaken. Once more, I recounted what I had seen. "Those metal pieces are probably shrapnel," he said. "When you go out again, try to stay under the roof of the barrack." He suggested that I rest my feet for a while before going out to report back.

A little later, I again took up my position near the fence of the hospital and stayed there for quite some time. The shooting came closer and closer. Then, all of a sudden, I heard a squeaking noise and realized that the big gate under the camp's administration building was being opened. I hid behind a fence post, afraid that the SS were returning. When I looked up again, I saw some soldiers get off a military vehicle and walk toward the center of the *Appellplatz* in the direction of the big gong. They did not look like the SS and wore uniforms I had never seen before. But I was still afraid to move. Then I heard the sound of the camp's gong. One of the soldiers was striking it as hard as he could, while another was yelling: "Hitler *kaputt!* Hitler *kaputt!*" They threw their caps in the air and performed what looked like a wild dance.

First one and then two inmates ventured out very carefully from the barracks where they must have been hiding. Others followed. Fearing that the SS had tricked them into believing that the soldiers were Russians, I waited to see when they would lower their guns and start shooting the prisoners. That did not happen. Instead, the soldiers embraced the first few men who reached them and seemed to be giving them cigarettes. By the time I got to the gong, a small group of inmates had surrounded the soldiers, who kept repeating that Hitler was "*kaputt*" and that we had been liberated. More people came out of their hiding places in various barracks. Again I looked all around, hoping to spot Janek and Michael, but they were nowhere to be seen. In fact, I never saw them again and never learned what had happened to them.

The Soviet soldiers who first entered Sachsenhausen had told us that we were free, that we had been liberated. I could not quite grasp what that meant. I had never really thought of liberation as such. My sole concern had been to survive from one day to the next. True, sometimes when lying in my bunk in the infirmary, listening to the sound of British and American bombers flying toward Berlin, I would fantasize that one of these large planes would swoop down, lower a big hook, pick up the entire barrack, and take it, with me in it, to England or America. That is something I could imagine, not liberation.

After the Russians had left, all of us who had greeted them around the camp gong started for the SS kitchen. I followed very slowly, some fifteen or twenty yards behind, always ready to take cover. I still could not believe that this supposed liberation was real and not some sort of trick concocted by the SS. *They probably staged this liberation in order to draw us out of our hiding places*, I thought to myself. That is why I did not walk into the kitchen with the rest of the men but kept my distance. When nothing happened, I slowly entered the building and on my way to the kitchen noticed an open door to what looked like an office. After making sure that no one was inside, I stepped in and looked around. Above the desk hung a photograph of Hitler; the walls were lined with filing cabinets; a telephone rested on the desk. I looked out of the window and saw a number of men going out of the kitchen carrying bread and some tin cans.

Maybe we really have been liberated, I thought as I climbed on the desk and pulled down Hitler's picture. I threw it on the floor, shattering the glass and the frame. I spat on it and stepped on his face so hard that my feet began to hurt, but still I went on until the picture was torn to pieces. Then I pulled out all the drawers from the filing cabinets and let the files fall to the floor. My work completed, I sat down behind the desk in the soft leather chair and picked up the telephone receiver. The line was dead, but I spoke into it anyway, telling my imagined listeners that Hitler and all Germans were dead. Then I pulled the cord out of the wall and limped over to the kitchen.

There the men were eating everything they could find. Some of them were hanging over big kettles, slurping what looked like soup the SS had left behind. The door to the storeroom was open, and a number of men came out carrying armloads of bread and sausages. Everybody was chewing on something. I found two loaves of bread, some onions, and a pickle. I began to eat the pickle, which was the only food I had an urge to eat at that moment and which tasted delicious, and limped out of the kitchen to share my "liberated" food with Marek in the infirmary. People were running back and forth out of the camp and into the kitchen — eating all the time while carrying more food. On my way out, a man pushed me and snatched one of my loaves of bread, but I was too excited to worry about it.

The news of our liberation had already reached the infirmary by the time I got there. Somebody had brought pails of soup and other food. Marek tried to tell everybody not to eat too much all at once because, being undernourished, they might die from overeating. But no one paid attention. Marek and I split the bread and onions and a remaining piece of the pickle.

In the late afternoon, a Russian officer came into our barrack. He told us that all sick people would be cared for by Russian doctors and nurses who were to arrive in a few days. Those who could walk were free to leave the next day. Marek called me over to his bed after the Russian had left. "We had better try to get out of here on our own," he said. "Who knows when the Russians will come and take us to a hospital. Besides, the Germans might reconquer the camp, and we don't want to be here when that happens. You'll have to help me get out of my casts." He produced a knife, and I started to cut. "Let's leave tomorrow morning, all right?"

I agreed, although I would have loved to have been taken to a Russian hospital on a Red Cross truck as the officer had promised.

When I woke up early in the morning, Marek was already practicing walking. "What a day!" he said, pointing to the window. "The sun is shining, celebrating our liberation. I had already given up all hope of ever again seeing my folks in Poland. What a surprise it will be!" And he performed an awkward jig. "Get ready," he said to me, "you are coming to Poland with me, and then we'll start looking for your parents." Yes, my parents. How I wanted to be together with them again! I did not know where my parents were, nor where or how we would be reunited. But even though I had seen many people die in the camps, it never occurred to me that my parents might not be alive. I was sure that they would find me as soon as they were liberated.

CHAPTER 7

Into the Polish Army

THE BIG SACHSENHAUSEN GATE WAS OPEN. Marek and I walked through it, under the administration building with its tower and the now-empty machine-gun nest near the area where some of the SS guards had been housed, and left the camp. We did not look back, either because we were afraid that some SS guards would suddenly give chase or because we did not want to be reminded of what lay behind us or both.

It took us a while to reach what looked like a major road or highway. It was teeming with tanks, military trucks, and horse-drawn wagons, carrying men and supplies. The men were waving to us and shouting. "Polish soldiers," Marek said, and we waved back, calling out to them in Polish. They threw us loaves of bread as they drove past, chanting anti-Nazi slogans and singing "Long live Poland!"

We had been told to travel away from the front, which was moving closer and closer to Berlin. That meant that we had to go in the direction from which the soldiers were coming. Along the way we met inmates from other camps. There was much waving and cheering, with everybody wanting to know what camp we came from. For a while the road resembled a street carnival. A Polish military truck offered us a ride to a nearby German town. "Most of the houses here are empty," the driver told us. "The Germans ran away because they are afraid of the Russians." Then, acting as though he owned the town, he added, "Move into any of these houses, and take anything you find there, compliments of the Polish Kosciuszko Division." The soldier laughed and drove away. As we walked down one of the streets, we met three Jewish girls from Hungary and two young men who had also just been liberated. They asked Marek and me to join them in the search for a house.

It did not take us long to come upon a large two-story brick house with a garden in front and a large backyard. It must have been abandoned on very short notice because the kitchen table was set, and there was even some food still on the plates. "Let's continue the dinner," one of the girls suggested. The cellar was stocked with canned fruit, vegetables, and even canned meat. We carried some of it up, and the girls started a fire and began to cook. What a wonderful dinner it was! My first real meal in years. The trouble was that while it all looked marvelous to me, I could barely swallow more than a few bites. Marek claimed that my stomach must have shrunk during all those years of near starvation. I did not know whether he was right; all I knew was that I could eat very, very little. Rather than stay at the table, I remembered the chickens and rabbits in the backyard; it had taken some persuasion on my part to save the rabbits from our eager cooks. I went out of the house to feed and play with the rabbits.

Wealthy people must have lived in the house, I thought. It had many rooms with fine furniture and paintings on the walls. It was hard for me to imagine, after Kielce, Auschwitz, and Sachsenhausen, that such homes existed and that families lived in them. The closets were filled with clothing. There were sheets and towels in drawers, as well as blankets and pillows. What would I not have given to have my parents with me in this house!

To the delight of the Hungarian girls, we found a sewing machine, and one of them immediately sat down to make herself a blouse with some material she had found. The men took all the clothing out of the closets and began to try on suits and pants. I found a pair of trousers, and since they were much too long on me, I simply shortened them with a kitchen knife and found a string to use as a belt. When I was all done, I threw my prison garb through the open window into the garden. Then I washed myself. *No more prisoner,* I thought, but then realized that the water and soap could not rid me of the one thing that would serve forever as a reminder of the concentration camp: the blue tattoo with my Auschwitz number on the inside of my left arm. Carefully, I dried my arm. *Papa will be proud of me,* I thought. Addressing him, as if reporting for duty, I called out, "B-2930 has survived the Ghetto of Kielce, Auschwitz, Sachsenhausen, and Germany! We won, as you predicted we would."

I enjoyed myself immensely in "our" beautiful house. It was very comfortable; I had a clean bed all to myself with white sheets, pillows, and a quilt cover. It reminded me of Zilina in Slovakia, of our apartment there, and the cozy bed I had in the

Grand Hotel. Through the windows of our new house, I could see Soviet tanks and trucks and soldiers, all moving toward Berlin. One day, while playing in the street, I noticed a Russian coming out of a nearby house. He was pushing a bicycle. *Oh, to have a bike!* I thought, and wondered whether I could still ride one. After all, I had not ridden a bike since I first learned to ride one in the Henryków factory in Kielce. Now I enviously watched the Russian soldier and his bike. As soon as he reached the street, he jumped clumsily on the bicycle and immediately fell off. He picked himself up and tried again and again. He started to swear, but the bicycle was unimpressed. I began to laugh. "Should I show you how it is done?" I asked in Polish, as I helped him pick up the bike. But he continued to swear. Finally, after yet another try, he threw the bike against the sidewalk and proceeded to kick it. "Don't break it, don't break it!" I cried, pulling on his uniform. He looked at me, spat on the ground, and walked away. That is how I became the proud owner of a bike. Of course, I jumped on it immediately and found, to my delight, that I had not forgotten how to ride.

The evenings in our house were lots of fun. Polish officers and soldiers dropped in and brought us food and candy. They asked about life in the concentration camps, wanted to know where we had been, told us about fighting the Germans and where they were during the war. Marek and I served as interpreters. They spoke of the conquest of Warsaw, the battles along the Vistula and Oder rivers, and the imminent German capitulation. Every evening more and more of them came. They told us about their regiments, and they showed me their decorations. One day a new group of soldiers came to visit us. They spoke with Marek and the Hungarian girls, while I was occupied polishing my bike, which I had carried into the house. The conversation dealt with Berlin and the prospects of victory. When Marek left the room to get some water glasses for the vodka they had brought along, the soldiers tried to communicate with the girls, but the girls did not understand Polish. I put my bike aside and asked them whether I could translate for them. "The girls understand German, and I speak Polish," I said.

Immediately, I became the center of attention. "A Polish boy!" they exclaimed, and before I had a chance to explain that I was not a Pole, Marek entered the room. "Yes, he is Polish," Marek said. "He was born in Kielce, and now I am taking him back." He winked at me. "Let's take him to Poland," one of the soldiers said. "He can come with us," added another. "I am staying with Marek," I said, and went back to polish my bike. When they had left, Marek came over to me and explained that it might not be such a bad idea to go with the soldiers. After all, they could take care of me better than he could and get me back to Poland faster. There I would soon find my parents. I was not at all persuaded and did not want to lose the only real friend I had.

Early the next morning, two soldiers came to visit. I knew one of them. He had been our guest the night before; the other was an officer. They had brought some chocolate and a bicycle bell. The officer introduced himself and told me that he had heard about me. "We are with the heavy artillery," he said, "and if you come with us, you'll have a great life." "Yes," the soldier chipped in, "you'll ride in military cars.

What a life! No more walking." "He's right," said the officer, "you'll have all the chocolate you want, and we'll let you
shoot the cannons." They talked and talked. Finally, in order
not to seem impolite, I promised to think about it. Then I
went out and attached the bell to my bike.

We had visitors again in the afternoon. Among the soldiers
who came, I recognized the two who had dropped by earlier.
They came into the garden and played with me. They showed
me all kinds of tricks I could do with my bike. One of them
asked me whether I wanted to learn how to shoot a gun. He
found an old can in the yard, took his pistol out, threw the can
into the air, and fired. It was a perfect hit. Then he gave me
the gun, placed the can on the fence, and showed me how to
aim. I was having a wonderful time. Another of the soldiers
gave me a penknife. Again, they began to speak to me about
returning with them to Poland. This time, somewhat to my
own surprise, I agreed. Suddenly, it all seemed very exciting.

The soldiers picked me up the next the morning. Parting
from Marek was not easy, but he assured me that I was doing
the right thing, and I wanted to believe him. I never saw or
heard from him again. My bicycle was loaded on the jeep, and
while my friends waved, we drove off. The car sped through
the streets of that little German town that had become our
temporary home. The jeep stopped in front of a large crowded
yard. "Here we are," said the driver. "This is the famous
Scout Company of the First Kosciuszko Division." The yard
was full of soldiers, trucks, armored cars, and horses. "Let's
introduce him to the captain," said one of the soldiers who
was holding my bike. We walked into one of the houses.

The captain was a tall, heavyset man whom I liked immediately. "This is Tomek," reported the driver. "Yes, yes," muttered the captain, "heard a lot about you." Picking me up in his arms, he immediately made me feel welcome. He then turned to one of the men and ordered him to get the company tailor and shoemaker. "We'll make a real soldier out of you," he said to me as he set me down again.

Within a day or two, I received something that looked like a Polish uniform, a belt, and a pair of shoes. Nothing seemed to be missing. The uniform had military buttons and even a corporal's insignia. "If you make a good soldier," the company tailor told me, "the captain will promote you to sergeant." I had become a full-fledged soldier, albeit in miniature: the mascot of the Polish army. I don't know exactly what date it was, although it must have been the end of April 1945. I was about two weeks short of my eleventh birthday.

At first, the tailor and shoemaker, who had made my uniform and shoes, were the soldiers I was closest to in the Scout Company. We ate all our meals together, and they soon noticed that I ate very little. That worried them, and they decided that they had to find a cure for my lack of appetite. When it appeared that the remedies they had come up with did not work, the shoemaker had an idea. "Why not try vodka?" he suggested. And out came the vodka. First a spoonful, then two, and finally half a *kieliszek* (tumbler), followed by little pieces of bacon. It worked like a charm: within days, I began to eat normally. This cure had the further consequence that, after a while, I could hold my vodka as well as many a soldier. I retained this capacity for vodka until my college days, when friends who had just seen the *Brothers Karamazov* movie bet me fifteen dollars—a lot of money in those days—that I could not drink a fifth of vodka, as one of the brothers had done in the movie, and jump over a chair. I won the wager but got so sick afterward that it was years before I could so much as look at a bottle of vodka again.

Besides showing me how to drink vodka and helping to revive my appetite, the tailor and shoemaker also tried to teach me their trades. I was particularly drawn to what the shoemaker called the "art of shoemaking," from the stretching, cutting, and sewing of the leather, to the nailing down of the soles with wooden nails. My new friend was a master at it, and as I watched him I thought that it would be fun to become a shoemaker. I still remember all the steps that went into the production of an entirely handmade pair of shoes.

Some days after I joined the Scout Company, we received orders to move on to Berlin. Despite the fact that we were probably stationed no more than thirty kilometers from the outskirts of Berlin, our progress was quite slow, since the company was not fully mechanized. While we had a few trucks, one or two cars, and a few armored vehicles, our supplies and maybe even the ammunition were transported on horse-drawn wagons, which brought up the rear and slowed down our advance. The roads were also crowded with advancing Soviet troops, whose tanks and artillery pieces kept passing us amid a great deal of shouting and general confusion. It was all very exciting to me, especially as I was permitted to ride in the armored vehicles, although I had to sleep in the horse-drawn wagons.

When we reached Berlin, the fighting for the city was still in full swing. Artillery and heavy machine-gun fire could be heard in the distance. Death and destruction were all around us. Most of the buildings along our route were burned out or reduced to rubble. The houses that were still standing were covered with bullet holes. Bodies of dead German and Soviet soldiers and of civilians were lying on the sidewalks and on the mounds of brick and cement that were all that remained of what had once been private homes, apartment houses, and office buildings.

Our destination was a park area not far from the Brandenburg Gate. The park was already largely occupied by Soviet troops with artillery pieces and *katyushas,* their rocket-propelled field guns. My company established itself in one part of the park, not far from the *katyusha* batteries, which made a terrible noise every time they were fired. I still remember one of the soldiers, probably a corporal or sergeant, who was in charge of a *katyusha* mounted atop a truck, hurling antifascist slogans and obscenities in the direction of the German defenders of the city each time he gave the order to release the rockets. Although the Germans seemed no longer to be firing their cannons in our direction, I was told to sleep in the armored car at night and to stay in it or near it during the day, because no one knew how long the Germans would continue to fight. Besides, there were still many German snipers around. A day after we arrived in Berlin, one of our soldiers was killed by a sniper shooting at a truck that had left the park to reconnoiter some suspected German positions.

As the fighting died down, some soldiers decided to go

fishing in a nearby pond and took me along. When we got there, one of them threw a hand grenade into the pond. Within minutes, the surface of the pond was covered with dead fish floating belly-up. My friends scooped up some fish in a bucket they had brought along. They called it "speed fishing." I don't know what they did with the fish, but if they cooked them, they did not share any with me.

I have only tried to fish a few times in my life and have never had much success at it. Once, on my first fishing outing with my sons, who were then still quite young, I cast my fishing rod with real gusto and, to my great shock and that of my sons, hooked the shirt of a fisherman standing on the other side of the pier. He did not look very happy when he realized what had happened. While I was trying to disentangle my hook from his shirt, my sons, fearing that the fisherman would attack me with the long knife hanging from his belt, kept moving ever farther away from me. But as soon as I told the fisherman that this was my first fishing experience, he burst out laughing and wished me better luck next time. At that moment, I thought of that Berlin pond back in 1945, which had actually been my first fishing experience—but certainly not the type of fishing I would recommend.

The news that Berlin had capitulated reached us a day after the "speed fishing" expedition at the pond. Of course, there was great rejoicing throughout our park, with shots being fired into the air from whatever weapons were handy. At the same time, vodka was being dispensed to the troops. Polish and Soviet soldiers could be seen embracing each other and sharing their vodka and cigarettes. Everybody was singing and dancing. A Polish soldier from our company gave me some swigs from his vodka bottle. The park had turned into a veritable carnival. As it got darker and the festivities gradually died down, I crawled into the armored car that had been my bed for the past few days and was soon fast asleep. That is how I helped liberate Berlin!

The war was still not over for about a week. My company, together with other units, was ordered to move out in pursuit of German troops that had retreated from Berlin. That day or a day later, we reached the edge of a forest. A whole German division was apparently dug in at that forest. Although they outnumbered us, their commanders were willing to negotiate an orderly surrender. The negotiations continued through much of the night. By morning, what had been expected to be a major surrender resulted in the capture of only the German officers who had taken part in the negotiations. The rest of the German division had simply vanished into thin air. After leaving the area around Berlin, we would from time to time run into groups of German soldiers who would surrender to us without putting up any resistance. It was quite an exhilarating experience for me to see German officers tremble in fear in front of us, when only months earlier they had inspired fear in all who had to appear before them.

A few days later, we learned that Germany had surrendered. The celebrations were even wilder than those that took place when we heard that Berlin had capitulated. The shooting and drinking continued for hours, into the night and even on the next day. The soldiers in my company were singing the Polish national anthem and all kinds of other Polish songs I had never heard before. Every so often, someone would raise his glass or bottle and drink to Poland and to the victorious Allied armies. Some soldiers stood around in small groups and spoke of home and of their families in Poland; others, with tears in their eyes, kept saying that they never thought they would live to see the end of the war and the defeat of Germany.

I was not sure whether to be happy or sad. Of course, I was happy that the war was over and that we had been liberated. But when the soldiers spoke of their families and of home, I was reminded that I did not know where my home was. I had no home without my parents, and I did not know where they were. I was sure that if I had survived, they must have survived too and that they would find me! In the meantime, my company was my home. But what would happen to me when all the soldiers went home? I decided that there would be time enough to answer that question, and for all I knew, it might never present itself since I was sure my parents would find me before the army was disbanded.

I had a wonderful time as we moved through Germany after its capitulation. Along the way, some soldiers from my company had come upon what remained of a German circus. There they found a beautiful pony and a miniature cart. They brought both to me, and one of the soldiers told me, "We liberated it for you. It needed a good Polish home." Now I spent many hours combing and feeding my new companion. I would ride the pony for fun, but when the company had to move, I would sit behind my pony in my little cart and follow the horse-drawn wagons that were carrying our supplies.

Along the way, soldiers from other companies would wave and shout to me as we passed. Before I got the pony, I had also acquired a small pistol of the type that women would carry in their handbags. I think it was my shoemaker friend who gave it to me. Since he had warned me that the five bullets in the magazine were the only ammunition he had been able to find for the gun, I shot it only once in order to find out whether the gun really worked. It did. From then on, I carried the pistol very proudly in a holster the shoemaker had made for me and polished it often.

We moved at a much slower pace through Germany after its capitulation than before, and we stayed for days in different towns. Many of the houses were empty, since their owners had fled in advance of the arrival of Soviet troops. We basically had the run of these towns. Some of the soldiers from my company amused themselves by breaking windows in the houses and causing all kinds of other damage. Encouraging me to follow their example, the soldiers would tell me that the Germans deserved that and more for all the suffering they had caused in Poland.

I did not see much excitement in breaking windows and preferred to play or to ride my pony whenever we stopped in a town for a few days. But one day a young soldier invited me to come along with him for some good fun. With his *pepeshka* submachine gun slung over his shoulder—this was a gun with a round magazine that almost all the Soviet and Polish soldiers used at the time—he guided me to a narrow street and pointed to the telephone poles lining the road. "See those white porcelain cups with the electric wires wound around them?" he asked. "We are going to try to shoot them down," he said, as he clicked a lever on the gun so that it would shoot only one bullet at a time. He had many misses but also some hits. When hit, the porcelain would shatter on the sidewalk, adding to the noise the *pepeshka* made. After a while, he handed me the gun. First, he had me aim it at a nearby fence "to give me a feel for the gun." It was not very heavy, and the round magazine seemed to help steady it. I had no trouble hitting the fence, but it took me a while to hit the targets on the telephone poles. I got the hang of it after a while. From then on, my friend and I would go hunting for these porcelain cups whenever we came to a new town. To this day, whenever I see telephone poles with porcelain cups, I recall, not without some shame, my acts of vandalism of long ago and feel a suppressed yearning to try it at least one more time.

Our meandering through Germany came to an end when my company, with all its equipment, was ordered to embark a train to Poland. The train stopped many times as we traveled, frequently alongside trains crowded with Soviet troops. We would then all get off our train and engage in friendly banter with the Russians. Poles and Russians would trade in all types of "liberated" items. The Russians would display their "*czassy*" (watches)—they would proudly show off four or five watches on each arm—and offer to trade some of them for other watches or jewelry. They seemed fascinated by what made watches tick. I remember one of them putting a watch under the wheel of a railroad car, while the train was being shunted about, to see what would happen to the watch when the car had gone over it. Everybody cheered when he retrieved the flattened watch and ceremoniously displayed the shattered pieces to us.

There were more cheers and much rejoicing when the train crossed into Poland. Our destination was a military garrison in the Polish city of Siedlce. There I shared quarters with a group of men from my company. The soldiers played a lot of soccer and cards as they waited to be demobilized and allowed to return to private life. There was also a lot of goofing around. A frequent pastime consisted of waiting until some unsuspecting soldier entered one of the outdoor privies near one of the barracks. A few soldiers then materialized out of nowhere, lifted the privy off its hole, and tipped the wooden structure on its side with the poor victim screaming and swearing.

At the garrison in Siedlce, I started to spend more and more time with a young soldier in my company who was Jewish. Over the years, I have forgotten the names of many people, but the name I most regret not remembering is that of this young soldier, although I still have the photograph he gave me of the two of us in our uniforms. While I imagine that many of the soldiers in my company guessed that I was Jewish, I kept that information to myself for fear, probably unjustified, that they would no longer treat me as one of their own. I did, however, tell my friend but asked him not to let the other soldiers know. Whenever we talked, he kept asking me what I planned to do in the future. Of course, I had no idea. I had not really thought about it, probably because I expected my parents to find me any day soon. He kept shaking his head, very delicately, trying to make me realize that it

Thomas Buergenthal (left) *in a tailor-made Polish Army uniform, with the soldier who took him to the orphanage, 1945*

would take them a long time to find me, assuming that they were still alive.

One day he let me know that he had to go away for a few days. He returned from his trip very excited and told me that he had found a wonderful Jewish orphanage in Otwock, near Warsaw. He had told the director about me, and she indicated that I would be most welcome to stay there until I found my parents. I would love it there, my friend assured me; I would meet many children my age who had also survived the war. Besides, our company commander had told him that a military garrison was not really the right place for an eleven-year-old boy.

A few days later my friend and I were on a train bound for Otwock.

CHAPTER 8

Waiting to Be Found

THE JEWISH ORPHANAGE OF OTWOCK WAS HOUSED in a white, longish, rectangular, two-story building, with a big front yard and a garden in the back. Surrounding it all was a thick pine forest where mushrooms, blueberries, and wild strawberries grew in abundance. A narrow paved road led to the orphanage from the town of Otwock. The orphanage could also be reached by walking through the forest along some well-trodden paths. Before the Second World War, Otwock was a well-known resort with many sanitariums where people suffering from tuberculosis could stay. Some of these facilities, converted to other uses during the war, lined one side of the road leading to the orphanage.

For me, the Jewish orphanage served as a halfway point from one life to another. It was here that I underwent a gradual transformation from being a perennially frightened and hungry camp inmate struggling to survive to an eleven-year-old child with a relatively normal life. I enjoyed almost every minute of my stay at the orphanage, although there were moments when I looked back with nostalgia on the adventure-filled life I had in the Polish army and wished I still had my pony with me.

The orphanage housed teenage boys and girls, as well as some younger children, separated into different groups. I was placed with the oldest group of boys. Here I was the youngest among some fifteen to twenty boys, which made me feel very important. Not all the children in the orphanage were real orphans. Some still had one or both parents. These children had been temporarily placed in the orphanage while their parents sought to reestablish their lives or were still abroad. I was among those whose parents, as far as we knew, had been killed during the war. We were the real orphans and saw ourselves as the orphanage's tough guys, lording it over the other kids. In some perverse way, our attitude resembled that of hardened criminals or "lifers" in a prison who take pride in their status. At the same time, of course, I continued to believe, without telling anyone, that my parents were alive and would find me one day soon.

The vast majority of children in the orphanage had been hidden during the war by Polish families or in convents. During that period, some of them lived under terribly difficult conditions. One girl, Tamara, who was my age, spent more than two years hiding in the low attic of a house. There was no room in that attic for her to walk or even to stand up. By the time she was liberated, her legs had become seriously deformed. Other children and their parents had managed to obtain false identification papers. This enabled them to pass themselves off as Poles in various towns and villages around the country, though they lived in constant fear of being denounced to the Germans. Some of these children were left to fend for themselves when their parents were caught in SS raids. Among the older kids, there were also some survivors of different German work camps. Each of us had a story to tell that was more horrendous than the next, but we rarely, if ever, talked about our past, although my friends loved to hear me regale them with tales of my life in the Polish army.

Since I was the only one in the orphanage who had survived Auschwitz, our administrators publicized this fact. As a result, I was frequently interviewed by journalists and trotted out to meet important visitors. I even appeared occasionally in the newsreels that were shown in Polish movie houses in those pretelevision days. From time to time, we were also visited by representatives of the American Jewish Joint Distribution Committee (the "Joint," as it was known), the organization that, I believe, was the orphanage's main benefactor.

We were treated very well in the orphanage. When I first arrived, I was examined by a doctor who decided that I was too thin for my age and needed to be put on a special dietary regimen to gain weight. For quite some time thereafter, my breakfast, in addition to the standard bread and boiled eggs, consisted of a bowl of light cream into which I usually stirred strawberry jam or orange marmalade. Some kids who were on this special diet did not like the cream we were served. Since I loved it, I frequently traded my eggs for their cream. Never before had I eaten so well! There were moments when, on seeing all that wonderful food in front of me, I felt sure that it

133

was all a dream and that, instead of the white cream I thought I saw, I would wake up and look down on the snow we ate on the Auschwitz Death Transport. In the late summer or fall, when the mushrooms in our forest were bursting out of the ground, our cook would send us out to gather them for her. For the next few days, we could count on wonderful mushroom soup or some special mushroom dishes. I thought I was in heaven.

When I arrived at the orphanage, I did not know how to read or write, apart from what my parents had tried to teach me surreptitiously in Kielce. I am quite sure, though, that I must have received some individual instruction from one of our counselors before I was sent to the nearby Polish grade school attended by the other kids from the orphanage. Curiously enough, I remember almost nothing about that school, how long I was there, what grade I was in, or what I learned. It may well be that I was there for only a brief period of time. But a couple of things stand out in my mind from my time at that school: the big crucifix that hung above the blackboard, and the daily prayer our Polish classmates intoned every morning while crossing themselves. Even though I did not participate in this exercise and was quite uncomfortable just standing there, I soon learned the words by heart and can to this day still recite them in Polish.

I also still remember the day I dunked one of Tamara's braids — she sat in front of me — into the ink pot on my desk. She gave me a terribly nasty look but said nothing to our Polish teacher. Instead, she reported me to the head counselor when we returned to the orphanage. A few days later, I was made to appear before an honors tribunal composed of some older kids. As punishment, the tribunal sentenced me to carry Tamara's books to and from school for a period of two weeks and to perform any other chores she cared to assign to me. That led to our becoming inseparable friends and, after a while, she even volunteered to mend my socks.

Much of our free time in the orphanage was spent on sports. It soon became apparent that, despite the amputation of my two toes, I could run very fast, and I gradually developed into a good soccer player. Since I could kick equally well with my left or right foot, I was able to play a number of different positions. As a result, I was always among the first kids chosen when the two best players of the orphanage selected their teams. In the orphanage I also learned to play table tennis, which was a big sport there, and after a while I could beat many of those who had taught me the game. At some point during my stay there, the orphanage created a boy scout team. Although we were still waiting for proper uniforms by the time I left, I very much enjoyed the activities we performed as scouts.

In the evenings, particularly on weekdays and after the Sabbath services, Polish and Jewish books would be read aloud. At times too, some of the kids would put on musical recitals. I remember that one of the older boys played the piano very well, while others sang or performed some other musical instrument. I soon learned, to my great regret, that I lacked all musical talent and could not even carry a tune.

From time to time, some of us older kids would be taken on excursions outside of Otwock or be allowed to travel as a group by ourselves. Once we were given permission to take the train to Warsaw, a mere twenty kilometers from Otwock. The occasion for our trip was the reopening of the main bridge over the Vistula River connecting Warsaw and its Praga suburb, which had been destroyed during the war. We had been given money for our tickets, and when we reached the station, somebody suggested that I buy the tickets, since I was the youngest and could claim that we were all under either ten or twelve, whichever the cutoff age was. When I got to the ticket window, I made myself shorter than I was and got the reduced-price tickets. We spent the extra money on candy and felt really proud of ourselves.

We grew vegetables in the garden behind the orphanage, and if we wished, we were assigned a small plot for individual cultivation. We grew cucumbers, carrots, beans, cabbages, and tomatoes. I loved working in my little garden, particularly after one of the kids showed me how to change the shape of a cucumber by putting the still-small plant into a bottle. After following his instructions, I would faithfully inspect my bottled cucumber every morning to see what was happening to it. My experiment did not turn out the way I had hoped because when I tried to get the ripe but deformed cucumber out of the bottle, I mutilated it.

To one side of our building, near the garden, the bee-keeper kept a row of beehives. Fascinated by what he was doing, I volunteered to help him one day. He instructed me on what to do, and, after donning the protective net he handed me, I tried to operate the bellows used to smoke out the bees so the beekeeper could remove the honey. As I struggled unsuccessfully to make the bellows work, I began to get stung on my gloveless hands and decided to run despite the beekeeper's warnings to stand still. The beehives must have been located some twenty meters from the orphanage building, and as I tried to outrun the bees, whole swarms began to follow me. With my protective net no longer in place, I was being stung all over my face and neck. I made it to the building and slammed the door shut, leaving most but not all of the bees behind. The nurse I went to see later said that I was very lucky, because had I been allergic to bee stings, I might well have died. As it was, I was in considerable pain for a number of days with my swollen hands, face, and neck. I never again went near the beehives.

One day two of my friends found a handgun in the forest, and they told me about it because, as they put it, I knew "how to handle guns." They had buried the gun near a tree and wanted me to look at it in order to see whether it worked. The three of us went into the forest, and my friends dug out the gun. I inspected it with all the apparent expertise I could muster for their benefit. It was quite dirty and even rusty in places, and I wondered whether it would work. What to do? Here we faced a real dilemma, for there was only one bullet in the magazine: if we tested the gun to see whether it worked, we would end up with a gun but no ammunition; if we decided to save our only bullet, however, we would always wonder whether the gun worked. Eventually, our curiosity got the better of us, and we convinced ourselves that at some future time we would be able to acquire the needed ammunition. Since I had bragged to all willing to listen that I had lots of experience shooting guns, my friends decided that I should be the one to try it out. I was not happy about this decision because I had been told by those who gave me my little gun in the Polish army that a dirty, rusty gun might explode when used. When it appeared that I had no choice but to demonstrate my expertise with guns, I asked my friends to stand some distance behind me as I proceeded to aim the gun at a big tree a few meters away. I pulled the trigger, and the gun went off with a big bang, emitting a great deal of smoke. But I was still standing, gun in hand and uninjured. We decided to rebury the gun after wrapping it in some cloth. We had planned to come back a few days later with bicycle oil or butter to clean the gun. In the meantime, though, Polish government placards appeared all over town, some of them nailed to trees near the orphanage, calling on the population to turn in all weapons. My two friends and I debated what to do with our buried gun and decided to leave it where it was. It is probably still there.

The mail for the orphanage had to be picked up at the Otwock post office in town. This chore was usually assigned to one or two of the older kids. They hated it, however, because to get to the post office they had to pass a nearby Catholic orphanage, where the Polish kids would bombard them with stones or try to beat them up while hurling anti-Semitic curses at them. Our kids therefore tried to avoid the Catholic orphanage by taking elaborate detours through the forest, although even then they might sometimes be set upon. Not long after I arrived at the orphanage, it was decided that because I did not look Jewish and could easily pass for a Pole, I should be given the job of picking up the mail. For a time, I passed the Polish orphanage without any problems. But once the Polish kids figured out that I came from the Jewish orphanage, I was no longer immune to their attacks. Although I could not escape their anti-Semitic cat-calls, I usually managed to outrun the Polish kids. The worst part of my job as mailman, though, was that there never was any mail for me.

During my stay at the orphanage, its administration was in the hands of the Jewish Bund, a leftist socialist political party that among other things believed that Jews should help build a socialist Polish state rather than emigrate to Palestine to help create a Jewish state. Those who ran the orphanage therefore made no effort to encourage emigration to Palestine or to engage in activities preparing us for it. This situation did not go unnoticed by some Zionist groups in Poland and prompted one of them—a Zionist youth organization known as Hashomer Hatzair—to infiltrate the orphanage in order to secretly promote emigration to Palestine. That is how a young woman by the name of Lola ended up at our orphanage. By the time I arrived at Otwock, she had become either the head counselor or the counselor for my group. While I am not sure what her precise position was, I know that I adored her, as did all of my friends.

After I had already been in the orphanage for some time, Lola invited me to go for a walk with her. As we left the orphanage grounds, she asked me whether I had ever thought of going to Palestine or whether I planned to stay in Poland. I must admit that I had never given the matter any thought, as I expected that my parents, whenever I found them, would make such decisions for me. Nevertheless, I had heard my father speak of Palestine and of the need for us Jews to have our own country someday. With his words in my mind, I told Lola, "I would love to live in Palestine because there I would not have to worry about being called a dirty Jew or have Polish kids throw stones at me." "If you are sure that you really want to live in Palestine," Lola said, "then I will let you in on a very important secret. But you must promise not to tell anyone."

After I promised her that the secret would forever be safe with me, Lola told me that some of the older kids, both girls and boys, had already let her know that they wished to live in Palestine and that she, in turn, would help them get there. She had drawn up a list with the names of these children, and if I was really sure that I wanted to move to Palestine, she would add my name to the list. Of course, I told her that I was more than sure. Lola then explained how the scheme would work. Starting soon, one child at a time would sneak out of the orphanage and be picked up by some people from Hashomer Hatzair. That child would then be taken to a temporary kibbutz in Poland, where arrangements would be made for him or her to be smuggled out of Poland to Palestine via either Italy or France. This process would be repeated every few weeks.

It all sounded terribly exciting. I immediately volunteered to be among the first kids to run away. But Lola explained that I had to be the last to leave the orphanage because I was "famous." What she meant was that since the orphanage administration had publicized my background and presence in the home, my disappearance would most certainly lead to investigations and jeopardize the entire operation. In the meantime, though, she promised that my name would be placed on the list and that it would be sent to the appropriate offices in Palestine. This way I could be sure that I would not be left behind. I was thrilled at the prospect of living in Palestine, and, though I was sorry that I would have to wait my turn, I accepted that what Lola told me made good sense.

Some months passed after that conversation with Lola without my hearing anything more about our secret. Then one morning, when I had given up all hope of ever moving to Palestine, the director of the orphanage called me to her office. Because we were usually asked to see the director only if we were guilty of some serious disciplinary transgression, I was sure that she had learned of the Hashomer Hatzair scheme and would interrogate me about it. On my way to her office, I worried about what I would say and decided that I would rather lie than risk revealing Lola's plans, which might get her fired. I certainly did not want to lose Lola.

A big smile greeted me when I entered the director's office. *She is trying to trick me*, I thought, *and get me to talk*. After asking me to sit down, the director began to question me about my parents. Did I remember my mother's name? "Gerda," I said. "What did you call her?" she asked next, and I replied, "Mutti." "Do you know where she was born?" I answered that she was born in Göttingen. There were more questions, some also about my father and when I had last seen my parents, and so on. I answered as best I could, still wondering what this was all about. Then the director asked me whether I would recognize my mother if I saw her. "Of course!" I said, and now I was totally confused. "What is this woman driving at?" I wondered and was sure that she would eventually get to the real reason for my being in her office.

Instead, the director pointed to a letter on her desk. "I have great news for you: Your mother is alive! This is a letter from her," she exclaimed enthusiastically. As soon as I saw the letter, all the excitement and happiness I felt at the news the director had just conveyed vanished. It was written in Polish, and I knew that my mother could not write Polish. The handwriting was also not hers. I knew that right away because, even before I knew how to read properly, my father used to make fun of my mother's handwriting by saying that it looked as if a chicken had walked over a piece of paper after stepping into a pot of ink. I knew that the letter the director handed me had not been written by my mother.

I felt like crying but did not want to let the director see how disappointed I was. I told her that the letter did not come from my mother and that it was probably written by someone who wanted to adopt me by pretending to be my mother. It was not uncommon for Jewish camp survivors, particularly those who had lost their own children, to come to the orphanage and offer to adopt us. Different Jewish organizations also encouraged adoptions in their publications. We older kids took special pride in refusing to be adopted, and since I for one was sure that my parents were alive and would soon find me, I had an even better reason to remain in the orphanage. The director tried to console me by suggesting that I might be mistaken about the letter. It could have been written in Polish for my mother by someone else, she suggested. After all, the letter was not addressed to me, she said, but to the orphanage, and my mother may have felt that a letter in German would not even be read. None of that convinced me, but as I ran out of her office in tears, I heard her say that she was not giving up yet and that I should not either.

Weeks passed. I tried to put the letter out of my mind but did not succeed. Because I was sure that the letter had not come from my mother, I began to wonder why, if my parents were alive, they had not yet found me, more than a year after the end of the war. Once I asked myself that question, I was forced to think the unthinkable: if so many other people were murdered, wasn't it possible that my parents had also died? No, that I was not willing to admit. It simply could not be true! Gradually, though, I began to have doubts and wondered whether maybe only one of them had survived. At this stage, I wondered whether, if only one of them made it, it would have been my mother or my father. I knew that my mother had had some health problems in the ghetto—I learned later that she suffered from a thyroid condition—and I also knew how good my father was at outsmarting the Germans. Those reflections convinced me that if only one of them had survived, it would have to have been my father. But if he survived, I thought, he would certainly have found me by now. In the past, before the letter, I had been able to avoid thinking about the fate of my parents by refusing to admit to myself that they might both be dead. Now it gradually dawned on me that I was probably all alone in the world and that there was not much I could do about it, other than go to Palestine. Suddenly, that prospect looked even more appealing.

Knowing that it would take some time before I would be able to leave the orphanage for Palestine, I tried to avoid thinking about my parents by spending more and more time playing soccer and table tennis. Then, one afternoon, while I was in the midst of an exciting soccer game, the director came running out of her office, waving a letter. I looked at it and immediately recognized my mother's unmistakable handwriting. It began, *"Mein liebster* Tommyli" — My dearest Tommyli. Right then and there I knew that she was alive. "She is alive!" I kept repeating to myself. It was the happiest moment of my life. I began to cry and laugh all at once, casting off the self-control and tough-guy attitude I sought to cultivate at the orphanage. I had a mother, and that meant that I could be a child again.

If it had been today, rather than in 1946, that my mother had learned I was alive, she would immediately have gotten on a plane or a train, traveled to Poland, and taken me back to Göttingen, her hometown, where she had returned after the war. But none of that was possible in 1946, nor was it possible for her to telephone me from Germany. Also, it would have taken my mother many months to obtain proper documents for travel to Poland. And since I had no passport, nor any other documents allowing me to leave Poland, more time would have been lost. It was thus readily apparent that other, less traditional travel plans had to be put together to get me to her in Göttingen.

In the meantime, mail was the only way for us to communicate. But in those days it was slow and not always reliable. It took some four to six weeks for a letter from Germany to reach me in Otwock, if not longer, which meant that we were probably not able to exchange more than a few letters before we were reunited. Once I knew that she was alive, I was naturally getting more impatient and frustrated waiting to be with her. I can only imagine what she must have been going through at that same time. Oh, how I would have loved at least to have been able to hear her voice!

It took more than three or four months for us to be reunited. Many people were involved in getting me from Otwock to Göttingen: the director of our orphanage, who was magnificent at pulling all necessary bureaucratic strings, and various Jewish organizations, among them the American Jewish Joint Distribution Committee and Bricha. The latter was a secretive Jewish organization that smuggled survivors from Europe to Palestine and, in the process, also helped reunite families dispersed throughout Europe. To this day, I don't really know who coordinated the various roles these organizations performed in getting me to my destination. What I do know is that my journey from Otwock, via Prague in Czechoslovakia and the American Zone in Germany, to Göttingen in the British Zone, with various stopovers along the way, was executed with admirable precision and without any hitches that I was aware of. It must have taken at least three weeks.

Such a voyage, even under normal circumstances, would have required considerable coordination, since I was passed from one group or individual to another at different stages of the trip. Not only did I have to cross a number of borders, I had to cross them illegally because I lacked the proper papers. Some people were responsible for the border crossings, others for putting me up in temporary or clandestine Jewish transit centers and at times even in hotels. On the whole, the border crossings were not very perilous and were sometimes effected in plain view of border guards who must have been bribed. Only one border crossing involved trudging in deep snow in the dark through a forest while trying not to get caught. I am no longer sure whether it was the Polish-Czech frontier or the border between Czechoslovakia and the American Zone in Germany. What I remember most clearly to this day, though, is the cold. This particular border crossing took place either in late November or early December, and my feet, sensitive to the cold because of my earlier frostbite and amputations, hurt and made walking difficult. That, in turn, brought back unpleasant memories of the Auschwitz death march. Fortunately, it took only a few hours to make this crossing before we arrived at a warm transit center.

With the exception of one border crossing, where I was the only person being brought over, I usually traveled in a group of between ten and twenty people — a "transport," as our Bricha guides called it. The composition of these groups and their size changed from way station to way station. For example, we would arrive at a transit center after we had crossed a border and find others already waiting there. That group would have priority over us in moving to the next destination, while we had to wait a few days more for our turn.

Although it was all very efficiently organized, it took a lot of time to transport us from country to country.

One event from that voyage was vividly brought back to me in a most dramatic way more than half a century later. In 1946, after having been smuggled from Poland to Czechoslovakia, I was detached from my group and taken to Prague. There, I was placed in the care of a young American woman who put me up for about a week in an elegant hotel where she lived. She was very kind to me, took me to nice places to eat, and showed me many interesting sights in the city. When the time came for me to leave Prague in order to join the transport that would take me to the American Zone of Germany, I promised that I would stay in touch. But I was not able to because, in the excitement of my anticipated reunion with my mother, I lost the piece of paper on which she had written her name and address. Then, on March 19, 2000, while working on my computer, an e-mail with the subject heading "Is it you?" flashed on my screen. The e-mail began with the following words: "I read in the *Jerusalem Post* of March 6 about your election to serve as World Court judge." After congratulating me, the writer continued:

> I am wondering whether you are the same "Tommy
> Buergenthal," who during the year 1946 or 1947 was
> brought from Poland to Prague, by special escort, and
> had to spend a few days in Prague, waiting...to rejoin
> his mother in Germany. If so, I was the welfare worker
> of the American Joint Distribution Committee, with
> whom you stayed and who took care of you. My name

then was "Freda Cohen."...Although more than 50 years have elapsed, I have never forgotten the child or the name "Tommy Buergenthal," and often wondered about your whereabouts. Seeing your name in print was a most exciting experience for me, and I would be very happy to hear whether you are in fact the same "Tommy Buergenthal."

The e-mail was signed "Freda (Cohen) Koren" and it came from Tel Aviv. Of course, I replied immediately. We corresponded for about a year and a half and made plans to get together as soon as possible. Then, shortly after she advised me that she intended to visit me in the Netherlands, I received the sad news of her sudden death; by then she was in her mideighties and had lived a full life. At the very least, I had still been given the opportunity, after all these many years, to thank her for taking such good care of me in 1946. While I had forgotten her name, I had of course never forgotten how kind she had been to me. I had also thought of her frequently, particularly when walking through revolving doors. This incongruous association between revolving doors and Freda, I explained in my first e-mail to her, was prompted by an experience I had when she brought me to her hotel. At the entrance of the hotel, I came to an abrupt stop in front of its revolving door. I had never before seen a revolving door, and it took me a while to figure out how one passed through such a contraption. "That was obviously one piece of information I did not need to know in order to survive in the concentration camps," I commented to her in that e-mail, as we tried to catch up on developments in our lives that spanned a period of more than fifty-five years.

After I left Prague, I crossed the Czech frontier with another transport and entered the American Zone near the Bavarian city of Hof, where another transit center awaited us. One more border remained, the one separating the British from the American Zone, before I would be reunited with my mother in Göttingen. I passed through that border in a U.S. military train, accompanied by another representative of the American Joint. The date was December 29, 1946. Göttingen was only some twenty kilometers away.

Once we had passed this last border, I got up from my seat and stood by the window until we rolled into the Göttingen railroad station. I could not contain my excitement. I spotted my mother even before the train came to a stop. As I try to describe the emotions of that moment, I realize that I am incapable of putting into words what I felt. And even now, so many years later, tears well up in my eyes as I see her standing there, nervously scanning the slowing railroad cars for a glimpse of me. While the train was still moving, I jumped out and raced over to her. We fell into each others' arms and stood there long after the train had moved out of the station, hugging each other and trying in just a few minutes to recount all that had happened to us since that August day in 1944 when we were separated in Auschwitz. "*Und* Papa?" I finally asked. She did not answer right away but kept shaking her head as tears ran down her cheeks. Right then, I knew that my father had not survived the war that was now finally over for my mother and me.

CHAPTER 9

A New Beginning

AS SOON AS WE WERE TOGETHER AGAIN, Mutti and I talked and talked for days on end about everything that had happened to each of us during the two and a half years we were separated. That is how I learned that in the fall of 1944 she had been sent from Auschwitz to the notorious women's concentration camp of Ravensbrück, located about ninety kilometers from Berlin. Ravensbrück was evacuated by the SS ahead of the approaching Soviet troops toward the end of April 1945. Mutti and the other camp inmates able to walk were marched in a westerly direction until they reached Malchow, a satellite camp of Ravensbrück. Many of the women died on that march. On April 28, 1945, Malchow was liberated by advancing Soviet troops. Ironically, at that point, a mere sixty-odd kilometers separated Mutti and me, yet it took about another year and a half for us to be reunited.

During the first week following her liberation, Mutti, together with a small group of her friends, rested in various deserted German houses they came across. There they also helped themselves to the clothing they needed and to food. Since, with the exception of Mutti, these women were all born in Poland, they decided to return to their hometowns as soon as possible in the hope of finding surviving relatives. Mutti joined them in order to get to Kielce, which was one of the meeting places she and my father had agreed on if they survived the war. She also assumed, correctly as it turned out, that others who had survived the Ghetto of Kielce would be returning to that city and would be able to provide information about my father and me in case we were not yet there.

Mutti reached Kielce after a horrendous journey on foot and by truck and rail that lasted almost two weeks. With no money and no food other than what little she could scavenge or beg from farmers along the way, she made it to Kielce totally exhausted. During the trip, particularly after her little group had split up, she had to be very careful not to be taken for a German. Since she spoke little Polish, she decided to claim that she was Hungarian whenever asked where she came from. She did not know a single word of Hungarian, though, and could only hope that she would not run into someone who would address her in that language. She was lucky on that score but, nevertheless, gave away her German origin on one occasion. That happened when someone stepped on her foot in the back of a very crowded truck. At that moment, a mild German curse escaped her lips. Before she knew it, she was pushed off the truck, fortunate not to have been beaten or worse.

A few dozen survivors had in the meantime returned to Kielce and established a Jewish community organization. Mutti was welcomed with open arms, since most of the people knew her from the labor camp and the Henryków factory. Provided with temporary shelter and food, she began to make inquiries about my father and me. She soon learned from other survivors that after my father and I had been separated in Auschwitz, he was sent to Flossenbürg and had died there shortly before the end of the war. For days, Mutti walked around in a stupor, unwilling to believe what she had been told. But as more and more survivors returned to Kielce and confirmed the news of his death, she had no choice but to accept it. (I found out only after the first edition of this book was published that my father had in fact been sent from Auschwitz to Sachsenhausen and from there to Buchenwald, where he died on January 15, 1945. Ever since I learned that our paths had crossed in Sachsenhausen, I keep asking myself, "What if we had been reunited in Sachsenhausen?" Yes, what if...)

None of the returnees whom Mutti approached could tell her for sure what had happened to me. Many of them knew me well from Kielce and Auschwitz, but no one had seen me after the liberation or near that time. One man thought he had seen me either on the Auschwitz Death Transport or in Sachsenhausen but was not really sure. As Mutti kept prodding them to remember whether they might have seen me after the liberation of Sachsenhausen, they tried to convince her that I could not possibly be alive. "None of the children survived," they would tell her. "How could he have survived?" they asked gently. "After all, he was by far the youngest from Kielce." "Now you must think of yourself and your health," they would add, concerned about her fragile condition and her nervous exhaustion. But she would have none of it. She knew that I was alive, for hadn't the fortune-teller proclaimed that I was a "lucky child"?

When her search in Kielce yielded no further useful information, Mutti decided that the time had come to travel to Göttingen, which was another of the meeting places she and my father had agreed on. Returning to Germany was no easier than her earlier trip from there to Poland. Conditions along the roads were still as chaotic and as dangerous as before, and transportation equally difficult to find. But with the help of some money she had received from the Jewish community in Kielce, Mutti eventually made it to Göttingen. She reached Göttingen totally exhausted and lapsed into a depression. She was hospitalized shortly after her arrival and treated for her now acute thyroid condition. The doctors also concluded that she needed total rest. In those pretranquilizer days, Mutti was placed on an extended regimen of sleep medication. She remained in the hospital for quite a number of weeks.

By the time Mutti left the hospital, she had regained some of her strength. It was not easy for her to find herself back in the Göttingen she remembered from her once-happy childhood and then the Nazi period. Almost as soon as the Nazis had come to power, most of Mutti's non-Jewish school friends acted as if they had never known her. They would cross the street when they saw her approaching or look the other way in order not to have to greet her. She was treated even worse the two times she returned to Göttingen from Lubochna to visit my grandparents and show me off, her new baby. Now, after the war, these same women embraced her on the street and acted as if nothing had happened in the past.

On the Gronerstrasse, one of the town's two main streets where my grandparents' home and shoe store had been located, the store's name— "Schuhgeschäft Silbergleit"— could still be faintly seen under the painted-over name of the new owner, to whom my grandparents had been forced to sell the house for a pittance. Mutti was born and grew up in that house, and now all that remained of that past and of her family's life in Göttingen were those rapidly fading letters spelling out her father's name. It is not surprising that in those early days in Göttingen, she frequently wondered whether having survived the camps was yet another punishment she did not deserve.

It was during that very difficult period, and as she agonized over the lack of any news of me, that Mutti was approached one day by an elderly woman who asked her to help her cross one of the busy Göttingen streets. Turning on the poor thing, Mutti screamed, "Nobody ever helped my mother across the street in this damn town!" and walked off. Years later, once the past had gradually lost its painful immediacy, Mutti would frequently recall her "shameful behavior," as she characterized it. It bothered her that she had been so terribly mean to that woman. "After all," she would ask, "how could I blame the old lady for what the Nazis had done to my mother?"

Not long after leaving the hospital, Mutti walked into the bakery next to where her parents' store had been. She was immediately recognized and lovingly embraced by Mrs. Appel, the baker's wife. Despite Nazi orders not to fraternize with Jews, the Appels continued to maintain contact with my grandparents until their deportation to Warsaw and helped

*The Silbergleits' home in Germany
with the shoe shop on the ground floor*

them whenever they could. After a happy and tearful reunion with Mutti, Mrs. Appel told her that she had something for her. She disappeared and returned a few minutes later carrying a dust-covered suitcase. "Your parents left this suitcase with us for safekeeping," Mrs. Appel told Mutti, as she handed it to her. "We were always afraid that the Nazis would find it and punish us, but we promised your parents we'd hide it, and we did." The suitcase contained some tablecloths and sheets, as well as a few pieces of silver. Near the bottom of the suitcase, Mutti found a batch of family photographs and some letters my grandparents had received from her and her brother, Eric, in America. For Mutti, the pictures were a treasure trove. All her family pictures, including photos of her parents, my father, and me, had been lost in the camps. Erased with the destruction of these pictures, it seemed to her, was proof that her family had ever existed. Now Mutti could again look at those images of a happier life long ago, before the Nazis destroyed it all. It was the first good thing that had happened to her since her return to Göttingen.

Housing was very difficult to come by in Göttingen after the war, despite the fact that the town had not been bombed. But that was precisely why the population of the city had almost doubled with an influx of German refugees who had lost their homes in the East. Mutti had been assigned an apartment, but she was not very happy with it because it was small and dark. Her problem was solved when she ran into Mr. Fritz Schügl. She knew him as the owner of a jewelry store that was located one street down from my grandparents' store. He wanted to know whether she needed a place to stay and offered her an apartment on the second floor of his one-family home. Housing and rentals generally were very strictly controlled in those days, but concentration camp survivors were given priority and were entitled to larger apartments. When Mutti moved into the sunny apartment with a large balcony overlooking the Schügl garden, her spirits improved dramatically and with them her health.

Throughout this period, Mutti never gave up hope of finding me. She contacted the many search bureaus in Germany and elsewhere that had sprung up after the war to help reunite families. She was also in touch with those Kielce survivors whose addresses she had been able to obtain, hoping to hear from anyone who had seen me or might have information about my whereabouts. In one of the letters she found in the suitcase Mrs. Appel had hidden for my grandparents, Mutti came across her brother's address in the United States and immediately got in touch with him. Until then, Eric did not know that his sister had survived or what had happened to their parents. He also learned that my father had not survived and that Mutti was still looking for me. Eric thereupon contacted various Jewish organizations in the United States and in Palestine, seeking their help in finding me.

Despite all the negative responses she received and suggestions from friends that I could not possibly be alive and that she should face this sad reality for her own peace of mind, Mutti insisted that I was alive. "I know that he is alive. I can feel it," she would say. It was only a matter of time "before I find him," she would tell anyone who tried to get her to face "reality." She was dramatically confirmed in that conviction by a blurred photograph she happened to see in a newspaper. According to the photo's caption, it showed a British soldier in Berlin walking with a group of liberated Jewish children. In that picture, Mutti was sure that she recognized me. "Here is the proof I've been waiting for," she told her friends, as she showed the picture to all who had doubted that I could have survived. Although I was in Berlin at roughly the same time, I never saw a British soldier in that city, nor was I one of the children in that picture. But Mutti did not know that at the time, which was good, for the picture sustained her in her belief that I was alive and gave her the hope she needed in those difficult days.

More than half a year after returning to Göttingen, Mutti learned that Dr. Leon Reitter, with whom she had worked in Henryków, had survived the war and was in a displaced persons camp in the American Zone, near the Dachau concentration camp from which he had been liberated by American troops. Born in Poland, he was a pediatrician who had received his medical education in Czechoslovakia because in those days only a limited number of Jews were allowed to study medicine in Poland. My parents and I came to know him in the Ghetto of Kielce; he was the doctor they called whenever I came down with a high fever or some other ailment that needed attention. Dr. Reitter and my father became close friends in Henryków and spent many hours in the evenings talking about the course of the war and what the future had in store for us. Dr. Reitter's only daughter was killed with the other children when the labor camp was liquidated. Mutti was, of course, overjoyed that Dr. Reitter was alive and invited him to Göttingen. Although it was not easy in those days to move from one zone of Germany to another, he eventually made it. Not long afterward, they decided to get married. When I arrived in Göttingen, Dr. Reitter was by my mother's side at the railroad station.

As soon as we reached the apartment in the Schügl house, I began to ask hundreds of questions, and so did Mutti. The questions just rolled out, and some of the answers produced tears, but we were impatient to know what the other had gone through in the years of our separation. I heard more details about my father's death, about Mutti's death march out of Ravensbrück, about Dr. Reitter's liberation from the Dachau concentration camp, and about the transport from Auschwitz to Germany that he and my father were on after we were separated. One group from that transport was apparently shipped to Dachau and the other to Flossenbürg.

Of course, I also wanted to know how Mutti had found me in Otwock. It appears that, true to her word, Lola, my counselor at the orphanage, had placed my name on the list of children who wanted to emigrate to Palestine. The list was transmitted to the Jewish Agency for Palestine. In the meantime, my uncle Eric in the United States had sent my name to a search bureau which that agency maintained. Despite the fact that millions of people were searching for lost relatives and friends, an employee of the Jewish Agency found, among the vast numbers of research requests received by his office, a letter indicating that a Mrs. Gerda Buergenthal in Germany was looking for her child. He then somehow remembered that, days earlier, he had seen the identical name on a list of children from an orphanage in Poland who wanted to be brought to Palestine. Considering that the person at the Jewish Agency was performing this search manually in those precomputer days, it borders on the miraculous that he managed in this fashion to make the connection between my mother and me. It is not surprising, therefore, that whenever Mutti told the story of how we were reunited, she would declare that it had been *"beschert"* (preordained). "After all," she would proclaim, "the fortune-teller in Katowice already predicted it."

The Jewish Agency immediately informed my uncle in the United States, who contacted my mother. Unable to travel to Poland after hearing that I was alive and afraid to write to me in German, Mutti had Dr. Reitter write to the orphanage in Polish. That was the letter I was convinced had been sent by someone who wanted to adopt me. In the meantime, at the request of my uncle, the American Jewish Joint Distribution Committee embarked on its efforts to reunite me with my mother.

Some ten years later, on her first visit to Israel, Mutti passed a building identified as the headquarters of the Jewish Agency. Without a moment's hesitation, she went in and asked to speak to someone in charge. She then explained that she had come to thank the agency for reuniting her with her son. While no one remembered the case of the boy in the Otwock orphanage who found his mother with the agency's help, she was given a joyous reception because, she was told, this was the first time anyone had come to thank the agency for bringing a family together.

CHAPTER 10

Life in Germany

WHEN I ARRIVED IN GERMANY at the end of December 1946, I was twelve and a half years old. During my first few days there, I did not let Mutti out of my sight. I kept kissing her and holding on to her, probably because I wanted to assure myself that I was not just dreaming and that we were really together again. It was such a wonderful feeling to be with my mother, to know that I was no longer alone in this world, that she loved me and would take care of me. Almost as soon as I first embraced her at the train station, I felt that a tremendous burden had been lifted from my shoulders and put on hers: now Mutti was again responsible for me. As I reflect on this attitude, I realize that it was probably a product of the selfish sentiments of a child: Until then, I had been responsible for my own life, for my survival; I could not afford to depend on anyone but myself; I had to think and act like a grown-up and be constantly on the alert against all possible dangers. But once I was back in her arms, I could be a child again, leaving these worries and concerns to her.

Portrait of Thomas taken in 1947,
shortly after his arrival in Germany

During much of the time I was separated from Mutti, I did not have many opportunities to speak German and lost some of my fluency. Within a week or two of coming to Göttingen, though, I was once again comfortable speaking German and even lost the slight Polish accent Mutti claimed I had acquired during my time in the Polish army and at the Otwock orphanage. It helped that young Fritz Schügl, the son of our landlord, lived with his family on the ground floor of our house. He was only two years older than I, and we became inseparable friends in no time.

From our balcony on the Wagnerstrasse, I could look over the garden on to the street below. The street—Hainholzweg—was a popular pedestrian route leading into the country-side east of the city. It attracted many Göttingen residents, particularly on Sundays, when entire German families would pass our house on their way to and from their walks. I would observe them from our balcony with envy and hatred. Here were fathers and mothers, grandfathers and grandmothers, walking with their children and grandchildren — people who, for all I knew, had killed my father and grandparents! As I contemplated these scenes of happy Germans enjoying their lives as if nothing had happened in the recent past, I longed to have a machine gun mounted on the balcony so I could do to them what they had done to my family. It took me a long time to get over these sentiments and to recognize that such indiscriminate acts of vengeance would not bring my father or grandparents back to life. It took me much longer to realize that one cannot hope to protect mankind from crimes such as those that were visited upon us unless one struggles to break the cycle of hatred and violence that invariably leads to ever more suffering by innocent human beings.

By the time I arrived in Göttingen, I probably had no more than half a year, if that, of formal education, all of it in that Polish school in Otwock. I was therefore not ready to be enrolled in a German school with children my age. After making some inquiries, Mutti found a retired high school teacher who tutored me for a little over a year. During that year, I made up the six or seven years of school I had missed. My tutor, Otto Biedermann, had been expelled from Upper Silesia when it was taken over by Poland and came to Göttingen as a refugee. He was a wonderful teacher who, probably more than any of the teachers I had thereafter, introduced me to the joy of learning. I would come to him every morning for a period of two hours, then work on the homework

*The balcony in Göttingen, where Thomas fantasized
about mounting a machine gun*

he would assign, which he corrected the next day. Initially, of
course, he had to teach me how to read and write—the basics
of what children learn in the first couple of grades—before
he could introduce me to all the other material I would have
learned if I had been able to attend school like other children
my age. That meant that Mr. Biedermann had to make sure
that I studied the following subjects, among others: German,
English, history, geography, and mathematics.

To improve my reading skills, Mr. Biedermann introduced

me to the books of Karl May, the famous German writer of Wild West books set in America that have captivated German children since the late nineteenth century, when they first appeared. My reading skills increased dramatically as I devoured these books, learning all about cowboys and Indians and the American frontier from an author who had never set foot in that country, but whose imagination and research made up for his lack of firsthand knowledge. His books were filled with suspense, making it very difficult for me to put them down. Once I had significantly improved my reading skills with Karl May's books, it proved easier for Mr. Biedermann to get me to read other books and thus, gradually, introduce me to the works of German literature that students my age had to read at school.

To improve my writing skills, he insisted that I write a brief essay every morning, describing what I had seen on my way from my home to his. Under normal circumstances, it would take me about fifteen minutes to walk to his house. Since I would soon run out of new things to report unless I varied my route, I got up earlier and earlier each morning to look for new ways to reach his home. On the way, I would see parts of town I had never seen before. I encountered all kinds of people in the streets and would try to guess who they were and where they were going. In those days, the streets of Göttingen, like those of other German cities, still provided ample evidence of the terrible human suffering the war had visited on ordinary Germans. I would see amputees, people whose faces had been disfigured by burns in the most bizarre ways, and some who had been blinded in one or both eyes. Many of these individuals still wore all or part of their faded military uniforms. I would pass people who, judging from their demeanor and clothing, looked like refugees. These daily discoveries made it easier to write the essays Mr. Biedermann demanded of me and led to interesting discussions about contemporary realities that I would never have encountered in school.

Mr. Biedermann once told Mutti that teaching me was an experience like none he had ever had. On the one hand, he told her, I was a child who lacked even the most rudimentary educational background and needed to be tutored as if I were a six year old; on the other hand, I had the life experience and maturity of a grown-up and could discuss subjects with him that no child my age would normally be aware of or interested in. While learning German and European history, I would ask him about life during the Nazi period and the reasons why he thought the Nazis had come to power, whether he had known any Nazis and what kind of people they were. I wanted to know about his expulsion from Upper Silesia and whether he blamed the Poles or Hitler for what happened to him and the other refugees. When studying geography, we talked about places I knew, countries I would want to live in, what types of people made up their populations, the foods they grew, and the animals that could be found there. Learning was fun with him, and I missed that sort of learning very much when I eventually entered school.

The only subject Mr. Biedermann did not feel competent to teach me was math—he had alerted Mutti to that fact and suggested that she find me a math tutor—but since I had no interest in or talent for math, I was pleased that we neglected that subject for some time until Mutti contracted a university student to provide me with the math background I needed to be ready for school.

When I returned to Göttingen for a brief visit a few years after emigrating to the United States, one of the first people I wanted to see was Mr. Biedermann. I had so much to tell him. He was interested in a great many things, and I knew that he would want to hear about my studies in America, about life there, about the books I was reading, and so on. When I called his home, I learned that he had had a stroke and was in the hospital. Of course, I went to visit him there. He recognized me as I walked into his room, and while he could not speak, he squeezed my hand and held on to it for a long time. I am sure that he knew that I had come not only to say good-bye but to thank him for laying the intellectual foundation for the life I was destined to live.

There were two high schools for boys in Göttingen in my time (in those days schools were still segregated by gender): one emphasized classical studies, such as Latin and ancient Greek; the other, which is now known as the Felix-Klein-Gymnasium, focused on modern languages and contemporary subjects. When Mr. Biedermann decided that I was ready for school, I opted for the Felix-Klein-Gymnasium and was admitted some time in 1948.* I was very pleased that I

---

*Unlike American high schools, German students in my day were admitted to high school after four years of primary school and a qualifying examination. They then spent nine years in high school.

was admitted to the grade that I would have been in had I entered primary school with my classmates. That made it much easier for me to become fully integrated into the life of the school.

I was the only Jewish student in the school. That had one great advantage: it meant that I was allowed to play in the school yard during the one or two hours a week that religion was taught. As a rule, a Protestant clergyman or theologian would teach this course to the Protestant students in my class, and a Catholic priest to the Catholic students. I was excused from the religion course because, it was explained to me, there was no rabbi in town to teach me. Of course, I was delighted not to have to attend any religion classes. Not surprisingly, some of my classmates envied my special status, since they too would have loved to have been excused from taking religion.

None of my classmates had ever met a Jew, but, as some told me later, they had seen Nazi cartoons depicting Jews as dark-skinned, alien-looking people with long crooked noses, black beards, and rapacious faces that were intended, because of their caricatured ugliness, to illustrate the repulsive character of Jews. That is probably why some of my classmates asked, on first learning that I was Jewish, whether I really was a Jew, for, as they put it, "You do not look like one." Others were surprised that I was good at sports, quite strong, and not afraid to defend myself when challenged by the class bullies. They had obviously been exposed to Nazi propaganda that described Jews as weaklings, cowards, and lacking all aptitude in sports. Soon, though, after the initial awkwardness and the novelty of having "a real Jew" in their class, I was accepted by my classmates as one of them, and, what is more, I gradually came to feel that I was indeed one of them. I never heard any anti-Semitic remarks from my fellow students, not even when I got into the typical schoolboy shoving matches with one or the other of them, nor did I ever sense that they harbored anti-Semitic feelings that they were hiding from me. But as I reflect now on those years, I am struck by the fact that I do not remember any of my classmates or my teachers asking about my life in German concentration camps, even though it was no secret that I spent the war years in these camps. Was it that they did not want to hear about my past, or did they believe that I would find it painful to talk about it? I do not know the answer.

Although my classmates accepted me, I could not help but feel that my presence made some of my teachers rather uncomfortable. Quite a number of them had been members of the Nazi party. After the war, they had to submit to the denazification process instituted by the occupation authorities and had to be cleared before they were allowed to teach again. I do not know how many former teachers had failed to pass this process, but the impression current at the time was that many a real Nazi—in contrast to the innocuous "*Mitläufer*," or "fellow traveler," one who had joined the Nazi party not out of conviction but for economic or other reasons—slipped through the denazification net and was reinstated. In these early postwar years, most of these people were afraid to voice their opinions. It was not surprising, therefore, that I was not subjected to any overt anti-Semitism, although I sensed that some of them were always on guard because I was in their class and because of their own past. They carefully avoided expressing their own opinions on certain "sensitive" issues that came up in class. I had the feeling, and that is all it was, that some of them may have been denazified without ever eschewing their Nazi views. Only once did some of these sentiments come to the fore. During a class discussion, and I no longer remember in which class it was, the teacher burst out with a harangue about the Allied bombing of Hamburg and the large loss of life. It was barbaric and unprecedented, he claimed. I raised my hand and asked, "What about the German bombing of London? Shouldn't we also speak about that? And what about all the people who were murdered in Nazi concentration camps?" Well, the man turned crimson and gave some explanation that equated the concentration camps to the Allied bombings, which prompted me to walk out of the classroom, a totally unheard of step in a German school in those days. My mother, of course, immediately complained to the school's director, and the teacher apologized in due course and said that I had misunderstood him. It was clear to me, though, that he apologized only for fear of losing his job. One of my mother's friends who had lived in Göttingen during the war chided her for not seeking the teacher's dismissal because the man was, as her friend put it, "*ein alter* Nazi" (a committed Nazi) who should never have been allowed to teach again.

We learned a great deal of history in our school, but it was mainly ancient and medieval German and European history. Contemporary history was simply ignored. Not only were the

Second World War, its causes, and the rise of Hitler never discussed but neither was the First World War, which, if I remember correctly, seemed too current a subject to be dealt with. That was in sharp contrast, of course, to the impressive efforts made in later years by the West German education authorities, who drastically revised their school curricula to permit and encourage students to confront the past honestly and to foster a democratic spirit of openness. Regrettably, that was not the case when I was at school in Göttingen. I was struck by the difference when I came to the United States and enrolled in an American high school in 1952. Being used to the oppressive discipline that in those days still reigned in German schools, I found the atmosphere in my American school almost too free and undisciplined. What most impressed me, though, was the freedom that American teachers tolerated and encouraged when it came to the expression of student views on almost any subject under discussion. We had a large number of student clubs and associations with elected officers in my American high school; a schoolwide student government with a panoply of officers; and annual elections for all those offices with election campaigns, pamphlets, and speeches mirroring American political elections. Whatever one might think of the academic quality of American high school education, the American classroom struck me as a veritable incubator of a democratic way of life, something the German classroom in my day certainly was not.

I spent a great deal of my free time in Göttingen on sports. I joined a table tennis club and a sports club, and played soccer to exhaustion with Fritz Schügl and other boys from school and from the neighborhood. I swam in the city's outdoor pool and in an abandoned stone quarry that was supposed to be off-limits. Fritz and I explored the countryside on our bikes and spent hours cleaning and oiling them. When I developed an interest in girls, we would join our classmates in the evenings, parading up and down the main street while ogling the girls and trying to arrange dates with them. There were parties and dancing and some drinking. In short, I lived the very normal life of a German teenager.

There were only a handful of Jews in Göttingen when I arrived there. Most of them were quite old. The unelected leader of this minuscule Jewish community was Richard Gräfenberg, the scion of one of the oldest, if not the oldest, Göttingen Jewish family, whose ancestors had received a *"Freibrief"* (license), allowing them to settle in the town as early as the late Middle Ages. Mr. Gräfenberg, who by the time I met him was very old, had been able to live peacefully in Göttingen throughout the war, apparently because his wife was not Jewish and also because she had good connections to the town's Gestapo chief. Gräfenberg had been able to keep his family home, which consisted of a large house and a beautiful garden with many fruit trees. From time to time, I was allowed to pick some of the apples, pears, and plums growing in his garden, a special privilege in those days of scarcity of almost everything edible. Mutti, who acted as Mr. Gräfenberg's deputy community leader—that sounds almost funny now, considering that there were probably no more than six or seven Jews in town, including us—had to visit him every month in connection with the distribution of the food packages the community received from the American Jewish Joint Distribution Committee. They had to be picked up from Hildesheim, the town's district seat, or from the former concentration camp of Bergen-Belsen, which functioned as a displaced persons' camp at the time. It was Mutti's job to make these trips, and I would occasionally accompany her. The packages contained not only food but also American cigarettes and coffee, both highly valued black-market currency items in those early postwar days. These could be traded for just about anything, from butter and meat to Persian rugs and jewelry. The people distributing the packages in Hildesheim and Bergen-Belsen not only tried to cheat us but would also suggest that Mutti was a fool not to claim that there were more Jews living in Göttingen in order to keep the surplus for herself. That would make her terribly angry, and on the way back she would always complain that the wrong people had survived the camps. It annoyed her even more when I reminded her that we too had survived. Of course, she was thinking of my father and would assert that, if he had lived, he would long ago have cleared those thieves out of the distribution centers. After Mr. Gräfenberg died, Mutti succeeded him as president.

As soon as I arrived in Göttingen, Dr. Reitter became my surrogate father. He was a gentle, kind, and most patient human being whom I came to love and admire. He helped me with my homework, taught me how to study, and encouraged me to read and to discuss what I had read. I was also very much attracted to his extensive medical library, particularly the anatomy and dermatology books with pictures of naked women, which I studied surreptitiously when neither he nor Mutti were around. Although Dr. Reitter had been a pediatrician in Poland, he decided to specialize in dermatology in Göttingen because, as he put it, "Pediatrics is too strenuous a medical specialty for someone with my heart problems," and he would add, "I no longer have the strength to make house calls." I had noticed that he would swallow some heart medication from time to time, particularly when we had to walk uphill from town toward the Wagnerstrasse where we lived. Once in a while he would take me to visit the university's dermatology clinic, show me the wards where patients with venereal diseases were housed, and explain how some of these diseases were contracted and what happened to people in the final stages of these ailments. I loved those excursions with him and decided that I would one day study medicine. In the meantime, I used to practice writing my signature in the German way with the doctor title—Dr. med. Thomas Buergenthal—I expected to earn.

Our excursions to these clinics became gradually less and less frequent. I noticed that whenever we had to walk up even the smallest incline, Dr. Reitter would have to stop often and take his heart pills. He complained of chest pain and found it increasingly harder to breathe after even the slightest exertion. As that pain got more intense, his cardiologist decided to have him admitted to the hospital; I believe he may have had a minor heart attack. Mutti, who had never had any experience with heart disease, thought at first that he was exaggerating the problem, but once she realized how serious his

Dr. Leon Reitter, 1947

condition was, she worried day and night about his health and threw all her nervous energy into his recovery effort. In those days before heart bypasses and angioplasties, doctors prescribed rest and more rest for his angina pectoris and mild heart attack, if that is what it was. Dr. Reitter was also given a variety of injections, but nothing seemed to help. Whenever I went to visit him, we would talk about his recovery prospects, which he felt were increasingly less promising. From time to time, he would draw a picture of the inside of his heart and show me where his blood vessels appeared to be blocked and why his heart did not get the blood it needed. Once in a while, when a nurse was very busy, he would show me how to give him an injection he needed — it was usually morphine — and I became quite good at dispensing it. Increasingly, though, he was getting weaker, particularly as water began to accumulate in his lungs and had to be drawn out with greater frequency. Then one day he told me that he would soon die and that it would be up to me to take good care of Mutti. But I was not to tell Mutti that the end was near. Not long after our conversation, Dr. Reitter died peacefully in his sleep. This was the second time I had lost a father and Mutti a husband. At that point we both decided that there was no God in heaven, for what kind of God would permit such a good man to die so young—he was only forty-eight years old—and cause so much suffering to be visited on one small family?

It took Mutti and me a long time to get over Dr. Reitter's death, if we ever did. Her thyroid condition began to act up again and with it her irregular heartbeat. We tried to console each other without much success, but we both knew that life had to go on and that we had to make the best of it. Our daily routine was interrupted one afternoon by an event that brought some happiness and excitement into our lives. Not long after I had arrived in Göttingen from Otwock, I told Mutti and Dr. Reitter about the Norwegian who had helped me so much in the Sachsenhausen infirmary and who probably saved my life. Although I had forgotten his name, I remembered that one day, when he brought me a jar of cookies he had received through the Swedish Red Cross, he pointed to the picture of a man on the side of the jar and said that it was his father. When Mutti heard my cookie-jar story, she suggested that the man whose son I knew in Sachsenhausen probably was a cookie manufacturer and that it was most unlikely that I would ever find him. But then, sometime in early 1948, Mutti saw an article in a newsletter published by an organization of former concentration camp inmates. The article reported that a Norwegian by the name of Odd Nansen, son of the famous Norwegian explorer and statesman Fridtjof Nansen, had recently published the diary he had kept in various camps in Norway as well as in Sachsenhausen, and that it had become the most widely read book in Norway.* After showing me the article, Mutti suggested that I write the author of the book and ask whether he could help me find the person who had been so kind to me in Sachsenhausen. I did just that. My letter to him began as follows:

Dear Mr. Nansen:

Please forgive me for disturbing you. A few days ago we read an article which pointed out that the most widely read book in Norway was your diary about your three-year incarceration in Sachsenhausen. I was also in Sachsenhausen. My name is Tommy Buergenthal, and I was ten years old at the time. I was in the *Revier*, where two of my toes were amputated.

---

*Odd Nansen's three-volume diaries, *Fra Dag til Dag*, were first published in Norway in 1947. English-language abridged versions of this book were also published in the United States (*From Day to Day*) and in Great Britain (*Day after Day*) in 1949. A much shorter German translation of the book (*Von Tag zu Tag*) was also published in 1949.

Then I told him about the Norwegian I had met there, that he had been very kind to me and helped me very much, but that I had forgotten his name and address. In the last paragraph of my letter, I reported that I had found my mother after a two-year separation, and continued:

> The name Nansen sounds most familiar to me, and that is why I am writing this letter to you. Could you possibly be that certain person? In case you are not, I would like to ask you to inquire among your circle of friends who that person could have been so that I might thank him.

Since I did not have the address of the author of the diaries, I simply addressed the letter to "Mr. Odd Nansen, Norway," and mailed it off.

Now the wait started. Weeks passed without an answer. In time I forgot all about the letter. Then one day our doorbell rang. When I opened the door, I was greeted by a Norwegian soldier who had arrived in a Norwegian military truck. (At that time, there was a small Norwegian military garrison stationed in the British Zone of Germany.) Pointing to the truck, he said that he had a package to deliver. When I suggested that he give it to me, he said it was too big for me to carry. At that point, two other soldiers jumped off the truck and opened its rear flap. They pulled out a huge wooden crate and carried it into the house, up the stairs, and into our apartment. "This is from Odd Nansen," one of the soldiers said, as he handed me a letter. The letter began with *"Lieber, lieber* Tommy!"* And it continued:

> You cannot imagine the great happiness your letter produced in me and many, many others....That is how we learned for the first time that you were alive and had found your mother. Your letter made your many old friends very happy, as well as the many new friends you now have without knowing it....First, I have to tell you that I am "that certain person" who visited you in the *Revier* in Sachsenhausen. Moreover, in my diaries, which you already know about, I devote a number of chapters to you and to our conversations in the *Revier,* where I met you and where I and many of my comrades came to love you and could never forget you. Many thousands of people have now read my diaries, and many of them think they know you because of that book. They have frequently asked me whether I had heard anything about little Tommy, but again and again I had to disappoint them.

Mr. Nansen then told me of his long and unsuccessful search for me, and his gradual assumption that I had not survived. But my letter changed all that. To know that I was alive and that I had been reunited with my mother was marvelous news for him, his family, and my many old and new friends. He asked me to write right away and to tell him all about myself and my mother and whether I had found my

ODD NANSEN

ARKTEKT

Angekommen den 7.II.48.

WERGELANDSVEIEN 7
TELEFON 33 02 64

OSLO, den 4.2.1948

Lieber, lieber Tommy!

Du weisst garnicht, welc\' grosse Freude Du mir und vielen, vielen anderen durch Deinen Brief bereitegt hast, wofür
ich Dir herzlichst danke. Erstens bekamen wir dadurch zu hören,
dass Du lebst und Deine Mutter wiedergefunden hast. Und für
alle Deine Freunde, Du hast nach und nach noch viele dazube-
kommen, wovon Du keine Ahnung hast, war es eine unsäglich grosse
Freude. Siehst Du, Tommy, das hängt folgendermassen zusammen:
Zuerst einmal war ich "der betreffende Herr", der Dich im Revier
von Sachsenhausen besuchte, und in meinem Tagebuch, wovon Du ja
selbst gehört hast, habe ich mehrere Kapitel um Dich geschrieben, um meine Gespräche mit Dir während der Besuche im Revier, wo
ich Dich kennengelernt und Dich, sowie viele andere Gefangenen-
kameraden so lieb gewonnen haben, dass wir Dich nie mehr verges-
sen können. Dieses Tagebuch wurde von Tausenden von Menschen
gelesen und vielen scheint es, Dich dadurch zu kennen. Sie haben
Dich natürlich genau so lieb gewonnen wie wir. Ständig haben sie
mich gefragt, ob ich nichts mehr über den kleinen Tommy gehört
habe, aber immer wieder musste ich sie durch mein Kopfschütteln
enttäuschen. Während der Zeit, die seit dem Kriegsende vergangen
ist, habe ich überall versucht herauszubekommen, ob Du nach dem
Kriege aus Sachsenhausen mit dem Leben davongekommen bist und wo
Du Dich zufällig aufhältst. Alle Nachforschungen waren leider ver-
gebens. Wir mussten nach und nach glauben, Du lebst nicht mehr.
Ich bin gerade auf einer langen Reisedurch Europa gewesen und
habe überall wo ich glaubte, es gäbe eine Möglichkeit, eine Spur
von Dir zu finden, Untersuchung eingeleitet, aber leider ohne
Ergebnis. Du kannst Dir deswegen vorstellen, wie gross die Freude
für mich war, Deinen Brief auf meinem Schreibtisch nach meiner
Rückkehr zu finden. Jetzt kann ich all denen, die nach Dir fragen,
mit Freude antworten und ihnen die leuchtende frohe Botschaft
überbringen: Tommy lebt! Tommy wohnt in Göttingen zusammen mit
seiner Mutter.
    Auch meine Frau und meine Kinder, ich habe vier Kinder,
sowohl älter und auch jünger als Du. Sie jubelten vor Freude,
als ich ihnen Deinen Brief laut vorleste, denn sie denkten auch
oft an Dich und wünschten sich so innig dass es gelingen möge,
Dich wiederzufinden. Und so lebst Du ja, sozusagen mitten unter
uns und hast noch dazu Deine Mutter wiedergefunden. Das klingt ja
wie ein unglaubliches, leuchtendes und gutes Märchen mitten in der
Elendigkeit in der Welt. Hätte ich nur gewusst, dass Du lebst und
in Göttingen wohnst, Du kannst sicher sein, ich hätte Dich auf
meiner neulichen Tur durch Deutschland aufgesucht. Ich kam auch
durch Hannover, welches ja nicht so schrecklich lang von Göttingen
liegt.

So gebe ich mich doch vorläufig mit der grossen Freude
zufrieden, die es für mich und für uns alle war als wir erfuhr-
ren, dass Du all das Böse und Schreckliche überlebt hast. Ich
habe einen Freund in Göttingen, einen Norweger, den ich darum
bitten werde, Dich aufzusuchen. Vielleicht kann er Dir auch
aus meinem Tagebuch, welches ich Dir senden werde, übersetzen,
wo ich um Dich geschrieben habe. So willst Du dann auch sicher
besser verstehen, warum wir alle so um Dich und Dein Schicksal
interessiert sind. Ich werde Dir auch Pakete schicken, Tommy,
mit diesen und jenen, was sicher von Nutzen sein wird. Das
wollen auch sicher andere gerne tun.

So musst Du mir nun, sobald Dich dieser Brief erreicht
hat, zurückschreiben und mir von Dir selbst und von Deiner
Mutter erzählen, und ob Du schon etwas über Deinen Vater gehört hast. Erzähle, wie es Dir geht, woran es fehlt, Beklei-
dung, Essen oder was es sonst sein kann. So wollen wir versu-
chen, es an Euch zu senden. Erzähle mir, ob Du fernerhin Lust
hast, nach Norwegen zu kommen. Ich könnte es vielleicht schon
so ordnen, dass Du mit Deiner Mutter hierher kommen kannst,und
ihr hier wohnen könnt. Du weisst, wir haben es doch in mancher
Beziehung hier oben in Norwegen besser als in Deutschland. _(ich weiss)_

Grüsse Deine Mutter von mir und sage ihr, sie muss doch
trotz allem glücklich sein, denn sie hat ja ihren lieben Jungen
wiederbekommen. Sage ihr, es sind so viele, viele, die sich
zusammen mit ihr darüber so sehr freuen.

Lebe wohl bis auf weiteres, lieber Tommy, Du wirst öfters
von mir hören und recht bald, hoffe ich, wirst Du dann auch
einige Lebensmittel bekommen. Jetzt werde ich mit Spannung auf
Deinen nächsten Brief warten.

                    Mit den herzlichsten Grüssen und Wünschen
                    für Dich und für Deine Mutter bin ich

                         Dein "Onkel"

                              Odd (Nansen)

Letter from Odd Nansen to Thomas

father. He also wanted to know whether we needed anything, particularly food and clothing, and he offered to help us move to Norway, where living conditions at the time were better than in Germany. The letter was signed, "Your 'Uncle' Odd (Nansen)."

As we started to open the wooden crate the soldiers had delivered from Mr. Nansen, I kept chiding Mutti. "I told you his father was not a cookie manufacturer! Nobody believed me that I would find him or that my letter would reach him. See, it reached him even without a proper address," I kept gloating. The crate was filled with the most marvelous food items: cans of sardines and herring, condensed milk, dried fruit, rice, flour and sugar, a variety of crackers, and many, many chocolate bars and other candy. Mutti and I just stood there in total disbelief. Who had ever seen so much food or even tasted it? At the time, food was still severely rationed in Germany, and even with the food packages we received from the American Joint, we never had enough, nor anything as "exotic" as this shipment. We were in seventh heaven and in the days to come ate more chocolate than was good for us. Later I learned that Norwegian schoolchildren had collected the chocolate and candy for me. They started this campaign after Norwegian newspapers reported that I was alive and living in Göttingen. Because Odd Nansen had dedicated his book to "the living memory" of some of his friends from camp and to "you too, little Tommy!" and had described me in his book as the "Angel Raphael of the *Revier*," I had become famous in Norway and something of a hero to the country's children. In the meantime, the three-volume book arrived with the following inscription:

Dear Tommy, here is my camp diary. As you will see, it is also dedicated to you. Even though you will not be able to read it in Norwegian, I want you nevertheless to have it as a present from a person who came to love you and one who never forgot nor ever will forget his young friend, that little brave angel from *Revier* No. III in Sachsenhausen.

Not long thereafter, Mr. Nansen came to Göttingen and arranged for me to visit him and his family in Norway. It was not all that easy for me to make that trip because I did not have a proper passport. Sometime after Mutti returned to Göttingen, she was offered her German citizenship back. She declined

"The Angel Raphael of the Revier,*"*
drawing by Odd Nansen

it, telling the official who had come to see her, "You took it away; now you can keep it!" That meant that we did not have a German passport and were only eligible for a stateless one. I eventually got such a passport and a visa for travel to Norway. Mutti and I met Mr. Nansen in Hamburg, from where he and I flew to Oslo. At the airport, Mr. Nansen introduced me to a German he identified as "my good friend, Mr. Willy Brandt, who fought against the Nazis in the Norwegian resistance." Of course, at the time, I had no idea who Willy Brandt was—I think he was deputy mayor of Berlin when we met. Years later, I would proudly claim that I knew Willy Brandt long before he became famous as West Germany's chancellor.

My trip to Norway was filled with one adventure after another. For one thing, I had never flown in an airplane before, which in itself was a thrilling experience. It was followed by a press conference at the Oslo airport, where I had to answer hundreds of questions. The Nansen family, including Mrs. Nansen and their four children—Marit, Eigil, Siri, and Odd Erik—treated me like a beloved, long-lost family member. Mr. Nansen also arranged for me to meet many former Sachsenhausen inmates who knew me from the camp, among them—if I remember correctly—a prime minister and other high government officials and leading personalities. I felt very important, of course, although I most enjoyed being able to swim with the Nansen kids in the Oslofjord, which abutted the Nansen family property. I had never even been near the sea, and the Oslofjord and the surrounding mountains were a very special experience for me. I also went with the Nansen family to their cottage in the mountains.

Thomas with Odd Nansen, 1951

Mr. Nansen was an architect by profession and an excellent painter. His camp diary contained many sketches of inmates and Nazi guards, and his home in Oslo was filled with these and other paintings and drawings. Fun conversations and reminiscences enlivened our dinners. I even learned some Norwegian words because it was decreed that one day a week the dinner language would be Norwegian, and if I wanted to eat, I had to ask for the food in Norwegian. That proved to be a strong incentive to learn the necessary words.

The trip back to Germany turned out to be most unpleasant. Some American friends of the Nansens were scheduled to travel by train to Copenhagen via Sweden on the same day I was to leave Oslo. The Nansens thought that it would be fun for me to have an opportunity to see Copenhagen, and especially the Tivoli, in the company of these friends as I made my way back to Germany. My plane ticket was traded in for a train ticket, and we were on our way. But I did not get very far. I was stopped at the border between Sweden and Norway. Since I did not have transit visas for Sweden and Denmark, which I needed as a stateless person, I was not allowed to proceed. That meant that I had to return to Oslo, where the Nansens obtained the necessary visas for me. Back in Göttingen, about six weeks later and without ever having stopped to see Copenhagen, I told Mutti what problems I had encountered with my stateless passport. She was quite upset that her stand on principle should now cause added hardship. "To hell with principle," she said, and a day later applied for the return of our German citizenship.

When the German translation of Odd Nansen's book appeared in 1949, he noted in the introduction that he was donating the proceeds of that volume to a fund set up to help German refugees. That made me wonder why a man who had spent more than three years in a Nazi concentration camp would care about the fate of these people. After some time, I began to think that it was important that individuals like Nansen and the rest of us who had been subjected to terrible suffering at the hands of the Germans treat them with humanity, not because we sought their gratitude or wanted to show how generous in spirit we were, but simply because our experience should have taught us to empathize with human beings in need, regardless of who they were. At the same time, of course, I was convinced that those Germans who ordered or committed the crimes the Nazis were responsible for should be punished, not Germans in general simply because they were Germans. That is why I also came to realize that the machine gun I wanted to mount on our balcony when I first arrived in Göttingen was a shameful idea. I concluded that even to contemplate that action reduced me to the level of those Germans who had killed innocent human beings. What is more, it dishonored the memory of those who had died in the camps. As time passed, these early random reflections came to solidify into convictions that influenced my thinking and actions later in life.

In 1951, shortly before I left Germany for the United States, Odd Nansen delivered a keynote address at an event organized to coincide with the conferral of the German Peace Prize on Albert Schweitzer, the famous humanitarian, by the Association of German Booksellers and Publishers. Mutti and I were invited to both events. The Schweitzer ceremony took place in the historic St. Paul's Church in Frankfurt. I knew, of course, who Schweitzer was and was very moved when Nansen introduced me to him. In his speech, delivered a day earlier, Nansen called on the international community to address the plight of German refugees. At the time, the question of whether Germany should be allowed to participate in the 1952 Olympics was still being debated around the world. In his speech, Nansen urged a favorable decision with the following words: "It is unjust and senseless to punish the children for the sins of their fathers. But that is what is sought to be done when Germany's young people are kept out of associations [designed to promote] international cooperation."

The theme of the conference, with its focus on peace and human dignity, had a profound impact on me in terms of the values to which I have devoted much of my life. I still have a dog-eared copy of Nansen's speech and a photograph of Schweitzer holding a kitten. Taking in the pomp and ceremony that surrounded us in that church—the first such event I had ever attended—I turned to Mutti, who was with me, and whispered, "Who would ever have thought that we would be allowed into this historic cathedral? Not all that long ago we were *Untermenschen* [subhumans], and now we are invited guests. If only Papa could be with us on this occasion." Over the years, I have thought often of my father when attending similar ceremonies in Germany and Austria. He who believed that Hitler and the Nazis would sooner or later be defeated never had the satisfaction, unfortunately, of seeing that he was right and witnessing the transformation of Germany into a democratic state.

Nansen came to Göttingen before the Frankfurt conference and told Mutti and me that he wanted to write a book about our camp experiences. He had apparently received many letters from the readers of his diary, urging him to tell my story in full. We agreed, of course, to be interviewed by Nansen for the book and spent a few days answering his questions. Although we remained in contact with Nansen in the years that followed, we heard nothing more about the book and assumed that he had decided not to write it. Nineteen years later, in 1970, his book *Tommy* was published in Norway.* He immediately sent me a copy. The long delay

Tommy: En sannferdig fortelling fortalt av Odd Nansen, published in Oslo by Gyldendal Norsk Forlag, 1970.

in getting the book out, Nansen explained, was due to the fact that in the intervening years he had been extremely busy in his architecture firm and had to put the book project aside. But, in 1969, he fell ill and was ordered by his doctors to give up his architecture practice. With time on his hands, he went back to his notes from the 1951 interview with Mutti and me and wrote the book. *Tommy* was published only in Norwegian. Nansen died a couple of years later without getting the book published in any other language. Fortunately, I saw Nansen before he died. While attending a human rights conference in Sweden, I decided to delay my return flight to the United States so I could spend a few days visiting him in Oslo. I did not realize how sick he was and was shocked to find him in such bad health. He refused to talk about his health and kept telling me instead that he was delighted that I was involved in human rights work. Of course, he did not want to hear that he more than anyone else was responsible for my choosing to embark on this career path. I learned only later that he was one of the cofounders of UNICEF. That did not really surprise me. After all, I was one of the beneficiaries of his lifelong commitment to helping children in need.

It was not until 1985, my final year as dean of American University Washington College of Law in Washington, D.C., that I was finally able to read *Tommy*. As my office was preparing the program for the last graduation ceremony I was to preside over as dean, I was asked by the president of the Law Students Association to permit him during the ceremony to say a few words on behalf of the graduating class. Of course I agreed, and when the time came, I invited him to take the floor. He walked up to the podium, unwrapped a package in a black binder, and told the audience that it was the English translation of *Tommy*. Explaining that *Tommy* was a book about my experiences during the Second World War, he continued, "Dean Buergenthal, the graduating class has commissioned this private English translation of *Tommy* as a token of our appreciation for you so that you will finally be able to read the book that tells your story." When I was handed the translation of *Tommy*, I just stood there, overwhelmed by emotion and unable to say a word.* It took me quite a while before I was able to continue with the prescribed graduation program.

During the years I spent in Göttingen, Germany underwent dramatic changes, particularly as far as the economic recovery of the country was concerned. The 1948 currency reform, which enabled us to exchange the largely worthless Reichsmarks for the new D-Marks, made a great impression on me because, almost overnight, empty store windows were filled with products I had never seen before. I think it was during that period that I ate my first orange. As I was eating it, Mutti told me that oranges were full of vitamin C and that, because they were very expensive and still difficult to obtain, they could only be bought when needed to ward off a cold or influenza. It was also about this time that I had my first taste of Coca-Cola. I don't know from whom or where Mutti obtained the bottle. Mutti showed it to me and told me that she had heard that it was a very special drink that quenched one's thirst with only a few sips and that I should

*No English translation of *Tommy* was ever published.

drink it only when I was particularly thirsty. She then put
the bottle into the cupboard—we did not have refrigerators
in those days—and there it sat until I came home one day,
terribly thirsty from hours of playing soccer. Mutti agreed
that the time had come to open the Coke bottle. The more
I drank that sweet, lukewarm drink, the thirstier I got. For
years afterward, I only had to look at a bottle of Coca-Cola to
be reminded of the unpleasant taste of my first sip.

We had many visitors to our home in Göttingen once
travel became easier in Germany. Some of them were people
we knew from Kielce who had heard through the grapevine
that we now lived in Göttingen. Others were foreign students
or professors who came to Göttingen to study. Some stayed
in the Fridtjof-Nansen-Haus, which had been founded after
the war by Olav Brennhovd, a Norwegian Protestant minister who ended up in a Nazi concentration camp for helping
to smuggle Jews from Norway to Sweden. He was a friend
of Odd Nansen, who introduced us to him. Brennhovd and
his wife became close friends and frequently brought greet-
ings from Nansen and other Norwegians who knew me in
Sachsenhausen. Another one of our early visitors was a young
British soldier who came to Göttingen as a war crimes inves-
tigator. Greville Janner was told about Mutti and me when
he asked to be introduced to Jewish families in Göttingen.
He soon realized that we were basically it. Greville was only
a few years older than I. We became good friends and have
remained in touch to this day. He served for many years in
the British House of Commons before being elevated to the
House of Lords. Lord Janner of Braunstone's lifelong efforts

on behalf of victims of the Holocaust probably date back to those early days in Göttingen and other German cities where he met many survivors.

The years I spent in Göttingen after the war were very important in helping me cope with my attitudes toward Germany and Germans. Those were not easy years for Mutti or me, and we often envied some of our fellow Kielce survivors who had ended up in Sweden right after the war. They did not have to face the economic hardships we faced in postwar Germany, nor did they have to struggle with the emotions we felt when contemplating the possibility that we were living amid murderers. At the same time, by living in Germany not long after our concentration camp experience, we were forced to confront those emotions in a way that helped Mutti and me gradually overcome our hatred and desire for revenge. Later, in America, I realized that many of my Jewish friends and acquaintances who had come to the United States before the war and thus escaped the Holocaust were much less forgiving than Mutti and I. I doubt that we would have been able to preserve our sanity had we remained consumed by hatred for the rest of our lives. Many of our relatives and friends in America never understood what we meant when we tried to explain that, while it was important not to forget what happened to us in the Holocaust, it was equally important not to hold the descendants of the perpetrators responsible for what was done to us, lest the cycle of hate and violence never end.

CHAPTER 11

To America

I ARRIVED IN NEW YORK on December 4, 1951. The ship that brought me to the United States was an American military transport, the USNS *General A. W. Greely,* one of the many so-called Liberty ships that had been mass-produced in the United States during the war. That was a fateful day for me. A new life was about to begin, and an old one had been left behind. But I did not know that at the time, for I traveled to America without a clear sense that I would settle there permanently. All I knew was that I wanted to see America—skyscrapers, big cars, Hollywood movies, chewing gum, cowboys and Indians. That was the America we kids in Göttingen imagined as we tried to find barbers who knew how to give American crew cuts, which had become the rage in my school. Of course, I looked forward to meeting my uncle and aunt, Eric and Senta Silbergleit—in America the name had become Silberg—and their daughter, Gay. I was to live with them in Paterson, New Jersey, less than an hour away from New York City. The very thought of being so close to Manhattan, Broadway, and the hundreds of movie houses I had heard about was all very exciting.

But those were by no means my only reasons for deciding to go to the United States. By 1951, at the age of seventeen, I was beginning to have doubts about remaining in Germany for the rest of my life. Although I was quite happy in Göttingen, I came to realize that I never really considered myself to be German the way my classmates, for example, thought of themselves as Germans. The term *Vaterland* (fatherland), which for the vast majority of Germans evokes patriotic emotions, triggered in me memories of Hitler and the Nazis; so too did the sound and words of the German national anthem. I was unable to shed these emotional associations, despite the fact that I was living in a very different Germany, a Germany that was being transformed into a solidly democratic state. These associations served as constant reminders of the crimes that had been committed in the name of the German *Vaterland*. The fact that I could not divorce the various nationalistic slogans and symbols from my past set me apart, in my own mind, from ordinary Germans and convinced me that in Germany I would always feel that I was different—different from that mythical "ordinary German." That feeling of not belonging or of being different was, of course, directly related to my past. At the time, moreover, I could still not rid myself entirely of the fear that the world had not seen the last of Nazi Germany. In retrospect, these fears seem to have been totally irrational. But in 1951, when I was seriously beginning to think about my future, only six years had elapsed since the collapse of the Nazi regime, and most of us who had survived the camps still could not quite believe that our nightmare was really over. These reflections and doubts about the future convinced me that I would never be able to put my past entirely behind me in Germany and that it would therefore make sense for me to emigrate at some point.

I was also forced to think about my future because my uncle and aunt in America kept urging Mutti and me to leave Germany and to settle in the United States. For a variety of reasons, Mutti was very reluctant to move to America. Her main worry was that she had no profession and that she would not be able to live in America on her German pension. That meant, she claimed, that despite her recurring health problems, she would have to work in a factory there. I do not know what prompted that idea, although the fact that my uncle and aunt had worked in various factories after they arrived in the United States in 1938 may explain Mutti's fear that a similar fate awaited her there. Whatever the reason, she became obsessed with that fear. It may well be that her decision to marry Jacob (Jack) Rosenholz, another survivor of the Ghetto of Kielce, was influenced in part by her worries about the life she thought she would have to live in America. At that time, she already knew that Jack planned to move to Italy, where he had relatives who wanted him to join them in a business venture.

For me the situation was very different. Although I was eager to accept my uncle and aunt's invitation to come to America, I did so without committing myself mentally to

*Thomas's aunt and uncle Senta and Eric Silberg,
previously Silbergleit, 1978*

making it a permanent move. In the back of my mind was
the idea that after a year or two in America, I might settle
in Israel. There was something romantic about the notion
of living in a kibbutz in Israel and helping to build a Jewish
state. More important, while I knew little about the realities
of life in Israel, I was sure that in Israel I would not feel "different," and that sense of belonging was becoming an important consideration in my thinking about the future. In short,

I really did not know what I would or should do in the long term; given my age, the long term seemed very far away. In the meantime, the thought of going to America, whether forever or only for a year or two, had immense appeal for me.

My decision to leave Germany for the United States was made much easier by Mutti's marriage to Jack Rosenholz and her willingness to move to Italy with him. Had that not been the case, I would have found it very difficult to leave her alone in Germany. Despite her remarriage, however, it was not easy for Mutti to face another separation from me. Although she agreed that I would have a better future in America and did not try to dissuade me from leaving Germany, she hoped nevertheless that I would be back in Europe within a year or two. At the time, I probably thought the same. During that entire period, Mutti and I had many a sleepless night wondering what we should do. Some of the problems we worried about, particularly lengthy separations, never really materialized. In the years that followed my move to the United States, I managed to visit her almost every second year by getting free rides across the Atlantic on freighters. On these occasions, I also managed to visit my friends in Göttingen.

Mutti had a wonderful life in Italy and was very happy there. And once I completed my studies and then married, Mutti and Jack visited us regularly. These visits became even more frequent after the birth of our sons. At that point, Mutti's interest in me shifted dramatically to her grandchildren. Now, as a grandfather myself, I understand that natural process, even though I viewed it with a certain amount of jealousy

Thomas and his mother in Bremerhaven in 1951,
shortly before his departure for the United States

mixed with a great deal of amusement at the time. I am also
very grateful that my sons still had the opportunity to get to
know their *"Oma,"* that very special woman.

After various inquiries about the bureaucratic steps I
needed to take to enter the United States, I learned that it

would make sense for me to seek admission to the country as an immigrant, rather than as a visitor or a student. It also appeared that I met the requirements to come to America as an immigrant under a special quota for refugee children. In those days, the United States still had a very strict quota entry system that depended on one's place of birth, rather than on one's nationality. Since I was born in Czechoslovakia, I would have fallen under the Czech quota, which had a long waiting list. By contrast, the refugee children's quota was wide open. I applied for a visa under that quota and received it after a brief wait.

A month or two later, I was asked to come to a transit camp in Bremerhaven, in the north of Germany. I stayed there for about two weeks, undergoing medical tests and various interviews by U.S. immigration officials. Mutti was with me throughout this time. She was happy for me, since I was excited about going to America, but very sad at the thought of not seeing me for a long time. In those days, America was very far away, and I can only imagine how difficult the idea of my leaving must have been for her. She kept giving me all kinds of motherly advice, from wearing warm clothes in the winter to eating well, and so on. The one piece of advice she gave me that still brings a smile to my face was "Remember, Tommy," she told me more than once, "it is better to have many girlfriends than just one. That will ensure that you won't get married too young." I was never quite able to comply fully with that advice. Mutti had also obtained a fifty-dollar bill on the black market, which was a great deal of money in those days. She told me to hide it in my shoe so that

Gerda in Trieste, 1957

it would not be confiscated on entry into the United States. She must have assumed that they had currency controls in America as they did in Europe at the time. I did as she said and can now only imagine what that bill must have smelled like on arrival in the United States, considering that the sanitary conditions on board our ship left much to be desired. Years later, when I read Emperor Vespasian's famous dictum that money does not smell, I remembered the fifty-dollar bill in my shoe. He was certainly wrong about *that* money.

My stay at the transit camp in Bremerhaven was largely uneventful. The camp was filled with refugees from all over Europe. Among them were large numbers of peasants and laborers from eastern Europe and the Soviet Union. Many of these people had been brought to Germany as slave labor or as prisoners of war. I later learned that this group most probably also included Nazi collaborators who had served as policemen and camp guards during the war and who now claimed to have been slave laborers in Germany. Another group consisted of individuals who had fled after the war from various eastern European countries that had been taken over by Communist regimes. Many of these people were professionals, including lawyers, professors, teachers, and medical doctors.

Since I spoke German and Polish and schoolboy English, I was called from time to time to act as interpreter for the interviews U.S. immigration examiners conducted with prospective immigrants. It did not take me long to realize that it was quite easy for those who claimed to be peasants and laborers to pass whatever test the examiners were applying for admission to the United States. Those refugees who had left their countries for political reasons and who were, on the whole, more educated were asked detailed questions about their backgrounds and political views. Judging by the questions the examiners kept asking, I soon realized that they were not really interested in finding out whether or not some of these prospective immigrants had been Nazi collaborators. They focused instead on ascertaining whether they were communists or had leftist leanings. It was only later that I learned that in the early 1950s, when the cold war was heating up and McCarthyism was at its zenith, the United States had admitted thousands of immigrants from eastern Europe, among them many who had collaborated with the Nazi occupation forces. Years later, when the U.S. government began to deport immigrants who had been found to have committed war crimes during the Nazi period, it was discovered that some of these people had managed to enter the United States because of sloppy screening by immigration authorities. I was not surprised.

The voyage to the United States took about ten days. I recently found among my papers a copy of the "Souvenir Edition of the Greely News," our ship's mimeographed newsletter. From it I learned that there were 1,271 refugees on board the *General Greely*. They were born in twenty countries and professed ten different religions. Roman Catholics were the largest religious group with 743 individuals, Baptists the smallest with two. There were fifty Jews on board, sixteen Buddhists, and eight Muslims; the remaining passengers represented various other Christian denominations. In many ways the passengers on my ship mirrored the immigration trends in the United States at that time. I had never seen people from so many different countries in one place and took lots of photographs of individuals whose faces suggested national or ethnic origins I had not encountered before. I was particularly fascinated by a Kalmyk family who looked Chinese to me but spoke Russian. They came from the Asian part of the Soviet Union and were also planning to live with relatives in New Jersey. I never did manage to find out how they ended up in Germany.

Most of our sleeping quarters were on the lower decks of the ship. We slept in single four-tiered bunks. The distance between each of the tiers was quite small, making it very difficult to sit up in bed. As soon as we arrived on board the ship, we were informed that we were all required to work, washing the decks, cleaning toilets, painting walls, and so on. I decided right then and there that there had to be more interesting jobs to perform and that I should try to find myself a more exciting assignment. As soon as I heard that frequent informational announcements were being made in different languages over the ship's public address system, I volunteered for that job and was hired for the German and Polish announcements. It turned out that I could also serve as one of the German-language editors of the ship's newsletter. With my two assignments came the right to work on the top deck in a very pleasant set of cabins. Since the ship's public address system was located on the bridge, I was also allowed to enter that part of the vessel, which was off-limits to the other passengers. Once they got to know me, the captain and the duty officers would allow me to linger on the bridge after I had made my announcements and would answer my questions about the navigational instruments on board. On one of those visits, Captain Niels H. Olsen, the ship's master, told me proudly that he had come to America from Denmark as a young man without speaking a word of English and that life had been good to him in his adoptive country. He assured me that I would be equally happy and successful in America.

I owe my introduction to American food to the chefs of the *General Greely*. Our meals were served in the mess hall on long, elevated metal tables. We ate our food standing up and had to hold on to our trays whenever the ship tilted to one side or the other. In rough seas, the trays of inattentive passengers would end up crashing to the other side of the hall. Our typical American breakfast consisted of ham and eggs, milk, coffee, and a small box of cereal. The cereal presented a problem for me and many others, for we had no idea what it was or how it was to be eaten. I finally decided that it was some sort of American dessert and carried the cereal box with me to the top deck, where I ate it like candy. I was by no means the only one who labored under this misconception, for the decks were usually full of passengers eating the dry cereal with their hands once breakfast was over. On one or two occasions we were given turkey for lunch or dinner. It was usually served with what I thought were carrots. Never having eaten sweet potatoes before, I could barely swallow my first mouthful. Not only did it not taste of carrot, my favorite vegetable, but it also reminded me of the turnips I had promised myself never to eat again if I survived the war. In time I came to enjoy sweet potatoes at Thanksgiving and Christmastime. On those occasions, however, they are prepared much more tastefully than the sweet potatoes the ship's chefs served us.

Our ship docked in New York harbor during the evening of December 3, 1951. We had to remain on board until the next morning. The New York skyline was ablaze with multicolored lights. On our way in, we passed the fully illuminated Statue of Liberty, which to this day symbolizes for me the warm welcome with which America received me as an immigrant. Seeing New York City at night is always a special experience, no matter how often one has had that opportunity. But seeing it for the first time after leaving a gloomy Europe still recovering from the devastation of a world war was truly a breathtaking experience. I will never forget that moment. As I looked out on that vast city glittering with what appeared to be millions of lights, many thoughts and images raced through my mind. I thought of that recurrent dream I had had in Sachsenhausen that one of the Allied bombers that flew over the camp on its way to Berlin would lower a big hook, lift up my barrack, and take me to America. That dream had finally come true, albeit not in such a fairy-tale way. I also wondered, not without some trepidation, what life would be like in America, when I would see Mutti again, and whether I did the right thing by leaving Göttingen. But the longer I stood at the ship's railing, fascinated by a sky drenched in the reflected colors of the multitude of lights that illuminated the city, I was transported back to Auschwitz and the reddish brown smoke bellowing out of the crematorium chimneys. Suddenly, the life I had lived—Kielce, Auschwitz, the Death March, Sachsenhausen—flashed before my eyes. Right then and there, I knew that I would never quite liberate myself from that past and that it would forever shape my life. But I also knew that I would not let it have a debilitating or destructive effect on the new life I was just about to begin. My past would inspire my future and give it meaning.

Epilogue

IN THE SIX DECADES since the end of the Second World War and my liberation, I have often wondered why or how I managed to survive the camps. These reflections are not brought on by feelings of remorse that I survived while so many others did not. Rather, my focus has been on the circumstances that allowed me to survive. If there is one word that captures the conclusion to which I always returned, it is luck. But luck is only the shorthand expression for a combination of factors that allowed me to make it. There was first the fact that during the ghetto and work camp periods in Kielce, I was together with my mother and father, who not only cared for me but also engrained in me the essentials of survival. Early on in Auschwitz, after I had already been separated from my mother, my father and I were still together. That allowed him to continue to protect me and to instruct me on ways to avoid ending up in the gas chamber. Of course, the fact that I was able to enter Auschwitz without being subjected to the deadly selection process on arrival was a major piece of luck.

Had there been a selection, I would never have made it into the camp, and that would have been the end of my story.

Once I was alone in Auschwitz and later on in Sachsenhausen, it helped that by then I was a little older and had become a true child of the camps in the sense that I had learned the tricks I needed to survive. I use the phrase "child of the camps" advisedly, because I have always felt that in many ways my survival instincts had much in common with similar traits I have observed in the "street children" of Latin America, who daily face many dangers and deprivations. These kids are frequently as young as I was or even younger. I point to these children when friends express surprise on learning how young I was. Children, even relatively young children, learn to be cunning or street-smart when circumstances demand, and they are fast learners when they have to be in order to live another day. When my own children were of the age I was during the war, I frequently wondered whether these pampered American children or the children of my friends could have made it in circumstances similar to mine. I am convinced that with some luck they could have, because the survival instinct in children is strong enough to allow them to adjust to the needs of their environment. Of course, what helped me was that I had a relatively long period of survival training. Who knows whether I would have survived had I arrived in Auschwitz from a normal middle-class environment and immediately had to face the brutal camp conditions. It was luck again that I had a gradual immersion into hell. (As I write these words I am not unaware of the bizarre use of the word *luck,* but that is what it was in its context.)

For my survival, I suppose it also helped that I spoke fluent, unaccented German and Polish and did not look Jewish. My German helped me on a number of occasions, as did my Aryan features; at least, that is what I think. Maybe I reminded some of the Nazi officers of their own children. This may have been a factor in the decision of the camp commandant of Kielce to let me live after I told him that I could work. Being able to speak Polish also proved useful on numerous occasions. Together, these things no doubt played a role in my survival and were entirely fortuitous.

At times I have been asked whether I ever suffered from the so-called survivor syndrome that allegedly afflicts some survivors who torment themselves for surviving when so many others, particularly members of their families, did not. Survivor syndrome has apparently driven some survivors to suicide and left others with serious psychological problems. I have never experienced these feelings. I don't know why, but if I were to speculate, I would attribute their absence to the instinctive belief of children in their immortality and their entitlement to live. It may also be that since I attributed my survival to sheer luck, I came to view survival and non-survival as a game of chance over which I had no control and was, therefore, not responsible for the outcome. How else to explain the fact that I did not catch diphtheria, even though I slept in the same bunk as my friend who came down with that very contagious disease? It could be argued, of course,

*Thomas in Auschwitz Birkenau, fifty-five years
after the infamous death march*

that my reliance on luck to explain my survival is itself a
defense mechanism against the mental ravages survivor syndrome is known to visit on survivors. And yet, it is no doubt
true that luck had a great deal to do with my survival.

I have also wondered from time to time why I can speak
and write very freely and, on the whole, unemotionally about
my camp experiences, while I am unable to watch movies
about the Holocaust or read books that deal with it. That is
not to say that in writing this memoir, I did not have moments
when I had to compose myself before going on. For example,
when describing the reunion with my mother or the killing
of Ucek and Zarenka, tears welled up in my eyes. Generally,
however, the story just flowed out of me. And though before
starting on this book, I was afraid that some of my Auschwitz
nightmares might return as I began to recall seemingly long-
forgotten episodes, that did not happen. By contrast, when

my children asked my mother to write down some of her Holocaust experiences, she started to write but had to stop after the first few pages. She told them afterward that almost as soon as she began to write, she started to cry and could not continue. Yet she could speak quite freely about these events. How to explain these quirks of the mind? Of course, the Holocaust robbed her of the best years of her life, and while she lived a relatively comfortable life after the war, it certainly was not the normal happy life she would otherwise have had or assumed she would have had. As she began to write down her war experiences for her grandchildren, the suppressed feelings about her loss no doubt reemerged. My own past did not really affect my future to the same degree.

Nevertheless, my camp experience has had much to do with my later professional life. Unlike most of my law school classmates, I was never really interested in the traditional practice of law, that is, in doing what lawyers do in most countries: defending or prosecuting criminals, representing clients in civil disputes, dealing with domestic relations matters, or otherwise providing legal advice to individuals and companies. Instead, I was drawn to international law and to international human rights law, as that branch of international law came to be known, because I believed, somewhat naively at first, that these areas of the law, if developed and strengthened, could spare future generations the type of terrible human tragedies that Nazi Germany had visited on the world.

Over time I also gradually concluded that I had an obligation to devote my professional activities to the international protection of human rights. This sense of obligation had its source in the belief, which grew stronger as the years passed, that those of us who survived the Holocaust owe it to those who perished in it to try to improve, each in our own way, the lives of others. To me that meant working for a world in which the rights and dignity of human beings everywhere would be protected. I also convinced myself that the international law of human rights was a field to which I, as a lawyer and because of my Holocaust experience, would be able to make a more significant contribution than to any other branch of the law. After all, I knew what it meant to be a victim of human rights violations.

That my Holocaust experience is never entirely removed from my professional work was brought home to me while dealing with a complaint submitted to the U.N. Human Rights Committee, on which I began to serve in 1995, by Robert Faurisson, a French denier of the Holocaust. Having been convicted by French courts for the violation of a French law making Holocaust denial a criminal offense, Faurisson challenged his conviction and the French law in a complaint filed with the Human Rights Committee. Given my personal history, I decided to remove myself from hearing the case. I did so with the following declaration: "As a survivor of the concentration camps of Auschwitz and Sachsenhausen, whose father, maternal grandparents, and many other family members were killed in the Nazi Holocaust, I have no choice but to recuse myself from participating in the decision of this case."

Before joining the Human Rights Committee, I had served on two major international human rights bodies: the Inter-

American Court of Human Rights and the U.N. Truth Commission for El Salvador. In many ways, they turned out to be my most exciting and productive human rights activities. The first of these began in 1979 with my election as judge of the newly created Inter-American Court of Human Rights of the Organization of American States. I remained on the Court, a part-time institution modeled on the old European Court of Human Rights, for the maximum two six-year terms and served as its president for the usual two-year period.

During the time I served on the Court, much of Latin America was ruled by military regimes and civilian dictators who were responsible for massive violations of human rights. While this was not a political climate in which a human rights court could count on the sympathetic support of many governments in the region, the Court was nevertheless able to lay a relatively solid foundation for the enforcement in the Western Hemisphere of the rights guaranteed by the American Convention. Our most important achievement during my time on the Court was the first ever international judgment holding a state—Honduras—liable for practicing a policy of forced disappearances. The government of Honduras was ordered to pay damages to the families of the victims and, what is more, fully complied with the judgment.

The Court's authority had been severely tested, however, in dealing with the Honduran Disappearance Cases. After testifying against the government, our first witness was murdered on a street of his hometown in Honduras. Another person whom the Court had decided to call as a witness became the next victim, under similar circumstances, before he ever had a chance to testify. To our relief, the killings of witnesses stopped as soon as the Court issued an injunction ordering the government of Honduras to ensure the safety of our witnesses, potential witnesses, and the next of kin of the victims of the disappearances. Our concern that the killing of witnesses would continue despite the injunction, with the government denying all responsibility, proved not to be justified.

During my time on the Court, we rendered important decisions relating to freedom of speech, the protection of human rights during national emergencies, due process of law, and related subjects. All in all, because of my interest in strengthening the development of international human rights law and institutions, I found my service on the Inter-American Court a dream come true. It is one thing to theorize about solutions to these problems but quite another to achieve concrete results that strengthen the protection of human rights.

The role that the Inter-American Court could play at the time was severely limited by the fact that some of the most serious violators of human rights in the region — among them Chile, Argentina, Uruguay, Paraguay, and various Central American countries — had either not ratified the American Convention or had not accepted the jurisdiction of the Court. These states could consequently not be brought before the Court. Thus, while we could hear charges against Honduras, which was alleged to have been responsible for some two hundred forced disappearances, we lacked that power for Argentina which, it was claimed, was responsible for between fifteen thousand and thirty thousand forced disappearances during its so-called dirty war. The fact that international human rights courts, international criminal courts, and similar bodies have jurisdiction over only those states that accept their jurisdiction, means that states that have not done so enjoy the very impunity these tribunals are designed to end. Sad, but unfortunately true. That is why it is so important, in my opinion, that all states become parties to the Rome Treaty establishing the International Criminal Court, and why I believe that the United States should ratify it. By not joining, the U.S. government is sending the wrong message to the international community about its commitment to the international rule of law.

As my service as judge on the Inter-American Court of Human Rights was coming to an end, the secretary-general of the United Nations appointed me to the three-member United Nations Truth Commission for El Salvador. Our charge was to investigate the massive violations of human rights that had been committed during El Salvador's twelve-year civil war, which had finally come to an end a few months earlier. Until then, I had always believed that my Holocaust experience had prepared me to deal with even the most egregious violations of human rights. In El Salvador, I found this not to be true. To see the skeleton of a baby still in the womb of a mother killed in the El Mozote massacre, where some five hundred women, children, and old men had been murdered, was more than I could take without being deeply affected by the utter depravity of those who committed this and similar crimes.

On entering the corridor of the residence of a group of Jesuit priests in San Salvador, I was shown the portrait of Archbishop Romero, a bullet hole near his heart. This symbolic reenactment of the archbishop's murder some years earlier was the work of the Salvadoran soldiers who, a few minutes later, went on to execute the priests and their housekeeper in the garden of their residence. The murdered priests' only "crime," I learned later, had been their desire to help negotiate a truce between the military and the guerrillas, something the leadership of the military feared. In El Salvador, we heard again and again that "orders are orders," and when we asked some of the military officers and the guerrilla commanders why they had committed or ordered this or that killing, we were invariably told that it was *"un error,"* a mistake. Never once during our interrogations did I hear expressions of remorse or admissions of guilt; mistakes yes, guilt no. How to explain that the intentional act of the killing of an innocent human being can be written off as merely a "mistake"?

El Salvador was a country in which many lived in fear. In this atmosphere, the victims or their next of kin often did not dare to speak about what had happened to them. People kept their suffering to themselves, hoping for justice but not really expecting it. For some people, ten years or more had gone by in silence with pent-up anger about the past. Finally someone—the commission—was listening to them, and the mere fact of telling what had happened was a healing emotional release. I was surprised to realize that despite their terrible experiences, most of our witnesses were more interested in recounting their stories than in seeking retribution.

One interview among many others comes to mind in this connection. It involved two women, one Salvadoran and the other either Swedish or Danish. They had come to the commission together to tell the story of their children. The son of one of the witnesses and the daughter of the other had met in Europe and had fallen in love. The couple traveled to El Salvador, became involved in leftist political activities, and were murdered by the military. Their mothers had not met until they decided to testify before the Truth Commission. They told us that they wanted to honor the memory of their children by telling their story together.

During our work in El Salvador, memories of my own past in another part of the world returned to me over and over again as we interviewed witnesses, heard their stories, and inspected the killing fields. The suffering that so many people in that small country had endured during its terrible civil war will remain forever imprinted on my soul. While in El Salvador, I often wondered whether the fact that I, with my Holocaust background, was investigating these crimes had some symbolic significance. Was it that these activities and my human rights work generally gave special meaning to my survival or that my survival compelled me, whether I knew it or not, to pursue these activities?

In the late 1990s, I found myself serving on the Claims Resolution Tribunal for Dormant Accounts in Switzerland. The CRT, as this tribunal came to be known, was set up to search for unclaimed Holocaust-related bank accounts and to help identify their owners or heirs. As its vice chairman, I had to supervise the CRT's day-to-day operations and to adjudicate claims submitted to us. In reading the claimants' applications and the bank files, my thoughts took me back to the 1930s, when some wealthy European Jews, vaguely sensing the fate that awaited them with the rise of the Nazis, sought to protect their money in neutral Switzerland. Many of them did not survive the Holocaust. That benefited the Swiss banks, which used the funds for more than half a century without ever accounting or expecting to account for their windfall.

Working with a group of commercial arbitrators from Israel, Switzerland, the United States, the United Kingdom, and Belgium, and a support staff of some twenty young lawyers, our job consisted of trying to determine whether the information provided us by individual claimants about deceased account holders matched the information found in the files of the Swiss banks. It was no easy task. Frequently, all we had to work with was the name of the account holder and, at most, a hometown or a profession. While I tried not to let my anger at the conduct of some banks affect the job I had to do, it was not always easy. For example, there would be bank files that contained nothing but the name of the account holder, the amount of money remaining in the account, and a notation that all other information had been discarded. Not only did the banks not pay interest, they frequently depleted the accounts entirely by deducting bank fees long after they must have known that the depositors had perished in the

Holocaust. There was evidence, moreover, that some banks had told Holocaust survivors seeking information about the bank accounts of relatives that no such accounts existed in the branch the survivors had identified, when they knew full well that the accounts existed in other branches.

There was always great joy in our offices in Zurich when we were able to connect the account of a Holocaust victim to an heir, but there were also moments of sadness when we learned that an heir had died before we had been able to make a finding of entitlement. Many heirs of account holders were never found. A case I cannot forget concerned an account claimed by a man and a woman in their seventies, living in different countries, who each contended that they were the sole heir of the account holder. After reviewing the case file, one of our young lawyers came to see me. He reported that the two claimants appeared to be siblings and that each believed that the other had perished in the Holocaust. I examined the file and agreed with him. The entire office was alerted, and there was rejoicing all around: we had not only found the heirs to an account but would also be able to reunite a brother and sister! Because of the advanced age of the heirs, we decided that the good news should be conveyed to them very carefully and that the brother should be contacted first. When I saw the face of the young lawyer shortly after he had made the call, I could guess what had happened: the brother had died three months earlier without ever learning that his sister was alive.

As chairman of the Committee on Conscience of the Washington-based U.S. Holocaust Memorial Council, it was my task to relate the experience of the Holocaust to contemporary realities by warning against new genocides and crimes against humanity. By the end of the mid-1990s, our optimistic assumptions that the world had seen the end of these crimes were belied by what was happening in Rwanda and in the Balkans. Before we had a chance to speak out and get the international community to act, hundreds of thousands of human beings had died. That was a familiar story to those of us who had survived the Holocaust. Although we worked very hard to get the international community to take action, that action often came too late, if at all, which only went to prove that we are still far from the day when "Never again!" really means what it is supposed to mean.

Over the years, contemporary events have triggered images in my mind of my camp experiences. During the Balkan conflict in the 1990s, for example, it was a common occurrence for TV stations to broadcast pictures of columns of exhausted refugees fleeing from combat zones. As I watched these scenes, I recognized myself in the frightened faces of the children. The pictures brought back memories of approaching German tanks on those Polish country roads, where our little group of refugees huddled in fear. When listening to the sole survivor of the El Mozote massacre, I was transported back to the liquidation of the Ghetto of Kielce and the shooting and screams that engulfed us as the sick and infirm were being murdered. At another point in El Salvador, while inspecting the courtyard of the residence where the Jesuit priests had been executed, I was told that the view of a distant observation tower that was relevant to my investigation was obscured by rose-bushes planted in memory of the priests. As I tried to look through the rosebushes, they gave way in my mind to the images of the beautiful wildflowers I had seen a year earlier on a visit to Auschwitz. The flowers covered the once barren ground of the camp as if to hide the horrendous crimes that had been committed there, just as the roses in that Salvadoran courtyard seemed intent on covering up the murders of the innocent priests. A few years earlier in San José, Costa Rica, I had a somewhat similar experience while hearing the testimony being presented to the Inter-American Court of Human Rights about the torture and killings that had been committed in Honduras in connection with forced disappearances. As I listened to the witness, I found myself remembering the brutal beating of Spiegel in that barrack in Auschwitz, the killing of the young Poles who had been caught looting during the liquidation of the Ghetto of Kielce, and the beating and subsequent hanging of the prisoners who had tried to escape from the Henryków work camp.

These and similar experiences have frequently accompanied me in my human rights activities. They have forced me to reflect on what it is that allows or compels human beings to commit such cruel and brutal crimes. It frightens me terribly that the individuals committing these acts are for the most part not sadists, but ordinary people who go home in the evening to their families, washing their hands before sitting down to dinner, as if what they had been doing was just a job like any other. If we humans can so easily wash the blood of our fellow humans off our hands, then what hope is there for sparing future generations from a repeat of the genocides and mass killings of the past? Was the Holocaust merely a practice run for the next set of genocides of other groups of human beings? Of course, I am very troubled by these questions, especially when I hear of new atrocities being committed in one part of the world or another.

These reflections might turn me into a cynic or have the effect of making me give up on my human rights work. But they do not have that effect. While I do not believe that I survived the Holocaust in order to devote my life to the protection of human rights, I believe that, having survived, I have an obligation to try to do all I can to spare others, wherever they might be, from suffering a fate similar to that of the victims of the Holocaust. It should therefore not be a surprise to anyone that the terrible crimes and cruelties experienced by human beings in many parts of the world since the Holocaust do not weaken my commitment to human rights. Instead, they reinforce my belief in the need to work ever harder to promote human rights education on all levels and to strengthen international and national legal and political institutions capable of making it ever more difficult for governments to violate human rights.

I also consider it a mistake to assume, as some do, that no significant progress has been made since the Holocaust in protecting human rights. The large body of international human rights laws in existence today and the many institutions established to enforce them, while they have certainly not put an end to all genocides or crimes against humanity, have tended to prevent or reduce large-scale human rights violations in many parts of the world. Here I think, for example, of the end of Apartheid and the emergence of democratic regimes in Latin America and elsewhere. The demise of the Soviet Union with its gulags is, in part at least, attributable to massive international efforts to put an end to that repressive regime. And who would have dared to dream in the 1970s or 1980s that eastern Europe would now be part of a democratic Europe? Admittedly, much still remains to be done, but the fact that some progress, however slow, is being made suggests to me that to give up hope now on efforts to improve the human rights situation around the world would only increase the suffering of an ever greater number of human beings and leave them without any prospect for a better future.

I tend to believe that had our contemporary international human rights mechanisms and norms existed in the 1930s, they might well have saved many of the lives that were lost in the Holocaust. The vast numbers of United Nations and regional human rights treaties, declarations, and institutions have created an international climate that expects governments to protect human rights and has made it increasingly more difficult for them to defend policies that result in serious violations of human rights. These laws and institutions have in turn contributed to the growth of nongovernmental human rights organizations that alert the international community to serious human rights violations almost as soon as they occur. Some democratic governments have over the years also developed national policies and practices that promote human rights on the international level. All these efforts have been helped by the contemporary communications revolution, which permits news of human rights abuses and unattended natural catastrophes to be broadcast around the world in almost real time. Mankind's yearning for human rights and human dignity has benefited from political and technological developments that gradually rob offending governments of the legitimacy and support they need to persist in violating human rights over the long term. That we can point to this or that government impervious to these developments proves no more than that progress is slow; it is equally true, though, that the number of such governments is decreasing, if only because in today's world these governments frequently pay a heavy political and economic price for engaging in practices unacceptable to large segments of the international community.

None of the international human rights norms, mechanisms, or policies to which I have referred here existed in the 1930s. The international law of that period allowed governments almost unlimited freedom to mistreat their own citizens. Nonintervention in the internal affairs of a state was the norm. It not only protected offending governments against international pressure but also provided other governments with an excuse for their inaction. Hardly any international nongovernmental human rights organizations existed at the time, and the world's media were neither equipped nor interested in stigmatizing violations of human rights. Today it is therefore easier than it was in the 1930s to arouse the international community to act. That does not mean that such action will always be forthcoming. But it does mean that we now have better tools than we had in the past to stop massive violations of human rights. The task ahead is to strengthen these tools, not to despair, and to never believe that mankind is incapable of creating a world in which our grandchildren and their descendants can live in peace and enjoy the human rights that were denied to so many of my generation.

Acknowledgments

THIS BOOK does not have the usual publishing history. I wrote it in English, but it was first published in more than half a dozen other languages. While this is not a unique situation, it is rather rare unless political, religious, or other reasons bar the publication of an author's books in his native country or language. That was certainly not true in my case. My problem, as I learned on more than one occasion from publishers in the United States and in the United Kingdom, was that "Holocaust books don't sell." It is therefore ironic that this book was first published in Germany in 2007 and that it remained on that country's bestseller list for quite a number of weeks.

It troubles me that some publishers in the English-speaking world assume that there is nothing more to be said about one of mankind's greatest human tragedies that their readers will want to read. If this assumption were to become a self-fulfilling prophecy, "Never again!" will lapse into a slogan devoid of the meaning it is designed to convey. We cannot hope to prevent future genocides and crimes against humanity unless we seek to understand the truth about, and the causes of, the Holocaust. Important insights about these questions can be gained not only from scholarly works but also from the memoirs of those who lived through it. I am therefore most grateful to the publishers of this book, Profile Books in the United Kingdom and Little, Brown and Company in the United States, for making my memoir available to the English-language reader.

My very special thanks and appreciation go to Andrew Franklin of Profile Books and to Tracy Behar of Little, Brown, for deciding to publish the book and for their insightful editorial suggestions. I also wish to express my admiration to Penny Daniel of Profile Books for so competently and pleasantly coordinating the publication effort between different parts of the world.

My agent, Eva Koralnik, of the Liepman Literary Agency in Zurich, Switzerland, deserves my appreciation for believing that my story should be published and for promoting its publication with enthusiasm and personal commitment.

At all stages of the writing of this book, I had the indispensable assistance of my secretary, Mrs. Danielle Touffet-Okandeji. I am profoundly grateful to her for the intelligence, professional skill, and, above all, helpful spirit with which she assisted me throughout the many drafts of this book.

My wife, Peggy Buergenthal, has lived through each page of this book and its many revisions. She has been my most severe editor and critic. As a result, she has enabled me to write a book that benefited immensely from her loving support, deep understanding, and creative editorial suggestions. In so many ways, this is therefore as much her book as it is mine.

About the Author

THOMAS BUERGENTHAL has dedicated his life to international law and the protection of human rights. He has combined a career as a professor of international law with judicial and investigatory activities devoted to the international protection of human rights and the rule of law.

Buergenthal served as the American judge of the International Court of Justice in The Hague from 2000 to 2010. On his return to the United States, he was reappointed Lobingier Professor of Comparative Law and Jurisprudence by the George Washington University Law School in Washington, D.C., a position he had held prior to his election to the ICJ.

Buergenthal's academic career began at the State University of New York at Buffalo Law School in 1962. There followed appointments as Fulbright and Jaworski Professor at the University of Texas Law School in Austin; Dean of the Washington College of Law of the American University, Washington, D.C.; I. T. Cohen Professor of Human Rights at the Emory University Law School; and Director of the Human Rights Program of the Carter Center in Atlanta, Georgia. He joined the George Washington University Law School for the first time in 1989.

Buergenthal has served as judge and president of the Inter-American Court of Human Rights as well as a member of the U.N. Human Rights Committee and the U.N. Truth Commission for El Salvador. He was chairman of the Committee on Conscience of the U.S. Holocaust Memorial Council and vice chairman of the Claims and Resolution Tribunal for Dormant Accounts in Switzerland. He is a member of the Ethics Commission of the International Olympic Committee.

Buergenthal graduated from Bethany College, West Virginia, and New York University School of Law. He earned Master of Law and Doctor of Juridical Science degrees from Harvard Law School.

Corecipient of the 2008 Gruber Foundation International Justice Prize, Buergenthal and his wife, Peggy, live in the Washington, D.C., area.

Reading Group Guide

A LUCKY CHILD

A MEMOIR OF
SURVIVING AUSCHWITZ
AS A YOUNG BOY

BY

THOMAS BUERGENTHAL

A *brief conversation with*
Thomas Buergenthal

You write in your book that you were "lucky" to get into Auschwitz.
What did you mean by that? What role did luck play in your sur-
vival during the Holocaust?

What I meant is that, unlike most people who arrived at
Auschwitz, there was no selection at the station. Had there
been a selection, children and old or sick people would have
been "selected out," that is, taken to the gas chambers.
Hence, I was lucky to have gotten into the camp.

Why did you wait so long to tell your story? Would your memoir
have been different if you had written it right after the war?

I waited so long because I was very busy raising a family,
teaching, writing law books, and doing many other important
things. Had I written the book right after the war, the book
would have dwelt too much on all the cruelties I witnessed
and been hate filled. In the process, the book would not have
focused on the issues I consider important.

What was it like for you when you returned to Auschwitz many years later? Were you surprised by what you found there?

What surprised me most of all was that the SS no longer recorded the names of the prisoners who arrived at Auschwitz in late 1943 and in 1944. All they recorded were the numbers that were assigned to us. That is when I realized that those who died in Auschwitz during those years died nameless, which struck me as a terrible indignity.

Your mother was such a remarkable woman. What qualities did she possess that helped her survive her ordeals? What was it like for you to find her again?

Yes, she was a remarkable woman. She had a magnificent resilience and an ability to successfully confront dangers on the spur of the moment. She was fearless and she had a great sense of humor that helped her cope. Being reunited with her was like entering paradise.

Odd Nansen, who went on to help found the organization UNICEF, became an important figure in your childhood after you met in the camps. How did his values and actions influence you?

He had a profound influence on me. He helped me recognize that hate and revenge had to be overcome if we wanted to build a world in which the crimes that were committed in the Holocaust would not be committed again and again against other human beings.

As *a justice on the International Court in The Hague, and as a jurist who has served on the Inter-American Court of Human Rights, you have borne witness in your professional life to numerous cases of crimes against humanity. How can we teach younger and future generations to work for equality and against hatred?*

I believe that the answer is to be found in education. We have to start teaching tolerance and respect for human life at a very early age. It has to be an education that focuses on the oneness of the human family and the beauty of its diversity.

How have your professional experiences changed you? What have they taught you?

My professional experience has taught me to respect the views of others, to reject the use of force except in self-defense, and not to assume that easy answers to contemporary problems are always the best answers. I have also learned to be patient and to listen more than to speak.

What are the core beliefs that led to the work that you do? Have they changed over time?

My core beliefs are based on the sanctity and beauty of human life as well as the belief that we have an obligation to ensure that human beings are protected against violations of their human rights wherever they might be. Yes, I have changed over time. I have become more patient in confronting life and more respectful of life.

Reflecting on Auschwitz
Six Decades Later

Adapted from an address that Thomas Buergenthal delivered on the occasion of the annual "Auschwitz Never Again" lecture organized by the Netherlands Auschwitz Committee, the Center for Holocaust and Genocide Studies, and the Pension and Benefit Board, January 27, 2009

I begin these reflections with the conviction that those of us who survived the Holocaust have a special obligation to make sure that the world not forget this horrendous human tragedy that will forever remain a blot on mankind's conscience. Annetje Fels Kupferschmidt, an Auschwitz survivor, lived up to this obligation by creating the Dutch Auschwitz Committee. It is therefore a particularly great honor for me to receive the award named for her. I do so also in the name of all those who believe in making "Auschwitz Never Again" the symbol of our commitment to a world in which all human beings can live in peace and dignity, with their human rights fully respected.

I was ten years old when I came to Auschwitz-Birkenau in 1944. There is much about the place I have forgotten, probably because I wanted to forget. The fact that I could forget is a blessing because it helped me preserve my sanity. But there is still much I remember, mostly the never-ending fear of dying and the constant hunger. As a child, I had to be especially afraid of the selections that Dr. Mengele, the Angel of Death, conducted with German precision, looking for more children, the sick, and the elderly to send to the gas chamber. Outsmarting him and living yet another day became a game I used to play, and every time I did not get caught in his deadly net, I felt victorious.

Hunger was my constant companion in Auschwitz. We got a little piece of black bread in the morning, if we were lucky, and a dark fluid that looked like coffee. The only other meal of the day I remember receiving was a very thin yellow-ish turnip soup and maybe, but not always, another piece of bread. I ate my bread as soon as I was given it, because if I tried to save it for later in the day it would invariably be stolen. As a child, I needed less food than the grownups, many of whom would on our diet gradually become Muselmen, as they were known, humans so thin that they looked like skeletons wrapped in a transparent skin. I don't know why they were given that name, but what I do know is that once they had become so thin, they had only a very short time to live. When they dragged themselves past me, I believed I was seeing dead people walking.

While in the Gypsy camp, where I arrived a few days after the Roma and Sinti who were housed there had all been killed—entire families, men, women, and children murdered!—I could on most evenings see the smoke and flames that bellowed out of the chimneys of the crematoriums. Each transport of new arrivals fed the flames of these monstrous ovens. Later, when I was moved to another set of barracks nearer to the crematoriums, I was close enough to hear the screams and pleas for help of the ever-increasing number of human beings who were herded into the gas chambers. At night, after a while, I could no longer separate their screams from the nightmares they brought on, and was afraid to fall asleep.

I also remember that during my time in Auschwitz the ground we walked on consisted of nothing but thick brown mud in the summer and icy slush in the winter. I never saw grass, bushes, or trees there. Nor did I ever see birds in the sky over Auschwitz. They stayed away because of the noxious smoke bellowing from the crematoriums that filled the sky. The birds could fly away; all we could do was wish that we could fly, and as the child I was, I believed that that miracle could happen. At night I sometimes dreamed that I was flying.

When I visited Auschwitz-Birkenau for the first time after the war, in the spring of 1991, I noticed that there were birds in the sky. Wildflowers and high grass covered the empty spaces where once had stood the many barracks that were torn down for firewood after the war. As I looked around, I could not rid myself of the feeling that this transformed scenery symbolized nature's way of covering up the terrible crimes that had been committed on this blood-soaked ground. And I began to wonder, not without some trepidation, whether nature would in due course play the same trick on our collective memories so that we would gradually not only forget the crimes that were committed in Auschwitz and elsewhere during the Third Reich, but also relax our vigilance against those forces and ideologies that have throughout history visited terrible crimes on mankind.

That must not be allowed to happen. Auschwitz and the part it played in the Holocaust must never be forgotten. By remembering Auschwitz we help ensure that men and women of goodwill will not let their guard down when some political movement, some tribe or government, is preparing to unleash yet another genocide in one part of the world or another, on one people or another. Only by not forgetting Auschwitz will we be able to make sure that our warning bells remain active and alert against this terrible crime. That is why "Auschwitz Never Again" is such an important event. To remember and commemorate Auschwitz is to commit ourselves to preventing other genocides in any part of the world. If we forget this commitment and the duty it imposes on us to value and protect human life, we will dishonor the memory of those who died in Auschwitz and the Holocaust.

On a recent visit to America, I showed my seven-year-old granddaughter Ruth the family pictures that are reprinted in my recent book, *A Lucky Child*, where I deal with my concentration camp experiences. She pointed to a picture of my father and asked who he was. I explained that he was her great-grandfather. Then she pointed to two other photographs and I told her that those were the pictures of my grandfather and my grandmother. She thought for a while and asked, "Where are they all now?" I replied that they had died. "Were they sick?" she wanted to know. "No," I said, "they were killed." "Why were they killed?" she asked immediately. I did not answer right away, not knowing quite how to reply. Finally I said, "They were killed because they were Jews." She looked at me and sounded worried when she whispered, "Mommy says we are Jewish." I took her in my arms and assured her that those terrible things happened in a faraway part of the world a long, long time ago when bad people tried to kill all Jews and many, many other human beings, but that we were safe now.

Afterwards I wondered whether those of us who survived the Holocaust really ever believe that we are safe. If the only crime that landed you in Auschwitz was that you were a child born of Jewish parents and that your father, your grandparents, and many other family members were killed because they too were Jews, what would justify your belief that genocides such as those committed during the Holocaust would never be repeated, given that the world stood by and watched as the Cambodia, Rwanda, and Srebrenica genocides took place? What guarantees do we have in a world in which these horrors occurred not all that long after Auschwitz, a world in which children are the first to die in wars, from hunger and disease?

Maybe some of us are safer today. But what about other human beings, other racial, religious, or national groups, different ethnic minorities — are they safe in the sense that what happened to us might not also happen to them in the future? These are the questions we must continue to ask ourselves; these are the questions that future generations must keep asking themselves if "Never Again" is to mean what it says.

We must believe that genocides and crimes against humanity can be eradicated from the face of the earth. And we must commit ourselves to the achievement of that goal.

I have written elsewhere that to speak of the Holocaust in terms of a number—six million—which is the way it is usually done, is to unintentionally dehumanize the victims and to trivialize the profoundly human tragedy it was. The six million number transforms the victims into a fungible mass of nameless, soulless bodies. It glosses over the fact that each of them was an individual human being—mothers, fathers, children, grandparents, artists, scholars, doctors, lawyers, people from all walks of life—with their dreams and hopes. Human beings each and every one, murdered in Auschwitz, Treblinka, Dachau, Buchenwald, Sachsenhausen, Bergen-Belsen, on the snow-covered roads during the Auschwitz death march, in the ghettos and the work camps, only because they were Jews.

I have often asked myself what the world would look like today had these individual human beings been permitted to live. How many potential Einsteins, Mahlers, Freuds, Kafkas, Werfels, Zweigs, and Chagals were murdered? What a reservoir of potential artistic, scientific, and intellectual creativity trampled under the storm troopers' boots and asphyxiated with Zyklon B gas! We will never know what contributions they might have made to mankind.

Reflecting on this terrible loss, we must recognize that the Holocaust was not just a Jewish tragedy; it was a tragedy for the whole of mankind. Millions of lives lost in many parts of Europe, so many cultures deprived of artistic beauty and intellectual greatness that might have been!

Of course, the same can be said with regard to the millions of human beings who have been murdered in more recent genocides. Think, for example, of the lives lost in the killing fields of Rwanda, Cambodia, the Balkans, and some other countries. In addition to the loss and suffering caused by the deaths of those who were murdered there, we shall never know what great intellectual, scientific, and cultural contributions they might have made to the world at large. Let us never forget that mankind as a whole is the victim whenever we permit a genocide to occur in one country or another.

As you know, Jews and Gypsies were not the only ones who were murdered in Auschwitz. Many thousands of human beings from all parts of Europe ended up in Auschwitz and in other German concentration camps, and many died there, either in the gas chambers or from hunger, executions, or beatings. Among them were resistance fighters, ministers of different religious faiths, men and women who all had the courage to oppose the Nazis even if it meant sacrificing their lives for their beliefs. They, too, must be remembered and honored whenever we commemorate the suffering that is synonymous with the Auschwitz name. In that sense Auschwitz must forever remind us of those who had the courage of their political and religious convictions, while shaming those who collaborated with a system that made Auschwitz possible.

The magnitude of the loss of life and destruction the Nazis visited on Europe is difficult to grasp. Millions of human beings were killed, maimed, made homeless, families destroyed, all because of a senseless war and racist ideology. Those of us who remember what Europe looked like at the time cannot but marvel at its subsequent transformation. But let us not forget how easy it was for the people of one of Europe's supposedly most civilized countries to follow or accept the murderous ideology of racial superiority that produced Auschwitz and Treblinka as well as a war that brought so much indescribable suffering to the entire continent and to many other parts of the world. In that sense, "Never Again!" must become a watchword for human beings around the world; it must be the clarion call for all future generations, reminding them not to permit a repeat of what happened in the 1930s and 1940s, and not to allow themselves to be misled or intoxicated by ideologies that advocate racial or religious hatred or ethnic cleansing, and that believe in the use of force to achieve their criminal objectives.

Over the years, I have often wondered how to explain the Holocaust and the genocide for which Nazi Germany is responsible as well as the terrible war it ushered in. The attempt to destroy a whole people, whole communities, whole nations, and whole cultures—all that will never be adequately explained, and I certainly have not been able to do it to my own satisfaction. It would be all too easy, however, to seek to justify the enormous crimes for which Nazi Germany bears responsibility by attributing them to a few demented leaders. That would exonerate many millions of ordinary Germans, who in one way or another were active or passive collaborators in these crimes, from their responsibility. The real German heroes were those Germans who had the courage not to compromise their convictions and who opposed the Nazi regime. Many of them paid the ultimate price for their beliefs and courage. They deserve our admira-. tion and respect.

Of course, it is only human to want to believe that no sane individuals could be responsible for intentionally causing all the suffering Nazi Germany caused. That normal, ordinary human beings rather than raving madmen share that responsibility is a truly frightening realization. It forces us to confront a reality few of us want to acknowledge: that ordinary human beings are capable, under certain circumstances, of committing or helping to commit such horrendous crimes. This fact compels the conclusion that others, in other parts of the world, may well be equally capable of supporting or participating in the execution of policies resulting in the commission of crimes similar to those of Nazi Germany. Maybe not on the scale or with the efficiency of the Nazi killing machine, but nevertheless with equally tragic consequences for the victims. How else to explain the genocides and massive crimes against humanity that have occurred with frightening regularity since the end of the Second World War?

We would all like to believe that only sadists are capable of committing such crimes, but history teaches otherwise. And unless we accept this sad truth and draw the necessary conclusions from it, we will never be able to prevent future genocides. That is why I consider this Auschwitz commemoration and similar events to be so important. Such ceremonies have an educational value that should not be underestimated, particularly if we believe, as I do, that no nation, no people have a monopoly on evil or on goodness. Without a proper education that seeks to draw the right lessons from the Holocaust, we will have little success in preventing future genocides in different parts of the world. Racial, religious, and political tolerance must be the watchword of this educational endeavor, and it must never be deemed to have accomplished its goal, if only because intolerance has a tendency to rear its ugly head again and again, if not in one country then in another. It is a cancer that lurks under the surface of all our societies.

Every generation must be reminded over and over again of the danger and causes of intolerance and of the crimes it nurtures. Our schools and universities must play a lead role in this effort. Unfortunately, much too little is done in this regard by the educational authorities in most of our countries. The important role played by institutes such as the Netherlands Center for Holocaust and Genocide Studies is therefore to be lauded and supported.

To remember Auschwitz without believing in and working for reconciliation with the Germany of today is to fail to recognize what contemporary Germany has achieved. Probably one of the most promising post-Holocaust developments has been the transformation of Germany from a militaristic, murderous Nazi state into one of Europe's leading democracies. Who during the Nazi period could have imagined the Germany of today? It is important, in my opinion, to acknowledge the democratic achievements of contemporary Germany, the positive role it plays in international relations today, and its efforts to bring about reconciliation with the victims of the Holocaust. Germany has admitted its responsibility and apologized for the terrible crimes it committed in the past. It has done so unlike some other countries that to this day have failed to ask for forgiveness for the crimes committed in their names. While the Holocaust must not and cannot be forgotten, Germany's efforts to atone for it are unique in history. These efforts must not remain unique; they must instead serve as an example to other nations. There can be no reconciliation without the good-faith effort to atone for past crimes. And there can be no end to hatred among nations and peoples without reconciliation and forgiveness.

As an Auschwitz survivor, I have had more than six decades to reflect on a subject that has been on my mind throughout all these years: the Holocaust produced many heroes and villains among the inmates of the camps, ordinary people who never lost their moral compass and those who became Kapos and barrack bosses and helped the SS torture and kill, frequently only for an extra piece of bread. For some, staying alive was the overriding concern regardless of the consequences, whereas others remained faithful to their religious or moral convictions, for which they were willing to sacrifice their lives. I wish I knew what drives a person in one or the other direction.

What I do know is that those human beings on either side of this moral divide cannot be easily identified ahead of time until they have to face the decision between good and evil. Is it upbringing, is it education, is it religion? I wish I knew, but I am convinced that our schools and our religious institutions and the state itself all have an obligation to instill into future generations the will and ability to resist aligning themselves with political movements and ideologies that advocate hatred. Tolerance and respect for other human beings regardless of their race, religion, national or ethnic origin, or sexual preference must be taught in our schools, in our military academies and religious institutions. Our political leaders, our governments, have an obligation to ensure that this be done.

That is why I believe that on occasions such as this, we need to remember and to honor the memory of one very special group of individuals. Here I think of the men and women of different nationalities and religions, including Germans, who risked their lives and their careers to save Jews during the Holocaust. Many of them are honored as the "Righteous among Nations" in the Yad Vashem Holocaust Museum in Jerusalem. But there were many more whose names and acts of humanity are lost in the history of those tragic days. The courage and convictions of all these individuals should inspire us and show us the way when yet another genocide threatens to undermine our moral beliefs. Permit me, therefore, to pay special tribute to the brave Dutch men and women who saved many Jews during the war and fought in the resistance.

None of our countries has done enough to honor individuals who throughout history have demonstrated great moral courage and conviction in fighting injustice, bigotry, and intolerance. Because our schools rarely expose our children to the inspiring humanitarian deeds of such individuals, they leave school knowing little about these heroes and the moral history of their countries. This history must be taught and valued. And there are many questions that should be asked while teaching it, particularly when dealing with the Second World War. For example, why were there so many collaborators in some countries in Europe and not in others, why did some resist and not others? How can we make sure that our sad past not repeat itself? Unless these and similar questions are asked, "Auschwitz Never Again" will remain an empty slogan.

As a child survivor of the Holocaust, I cannot end this talk today without asking you to remember the hundreds of thousands of children who were murdered in the Holocaust. Many of them would still be alive today had they been permitted to live out their lives: the Anne Franks, the Petr Ginzes, Ucek and Zarenka, my little adoptive brother and sister, and many, many others. And let us not forget the children who are killed or die of starvation in never-ending armed conflicts, those who were murdered in Rwanda, in the Balkans, in Cambodia, who will keep dying in other parts of the world unless and until we can create a world in which "Never Again" really means "Never Again" and not "Never Again until the next time."

Questions and topics for discussion

1. Thomas Buergenthal says that he tried to write his story "as I remember living it as the child I was, not as an old man reflecting on that life" (page xvii). How do you think the effort to achieve this perspective shaped the book? What effect might writing *A Lucky Child* through the eyes of an adult have had on the narrative? What thoughts, ideas, and emotions are added or taken away when writing about such a defining life experience through the eyes of a child?

2. Young Thomas was forced to leave his beloved little red car behind when the Buergenthals' hotel in Lubochna was occupied by Slovak allies of Nazi Germany—a heartbreak he never forgot. Were you ever forced to give up something as a child that you could never forget, even if it seemed silly in the face of greater losses?

3. Thomas's mother insisted for the rest of her life that the fortune-teller was correct in her prediction that her

son was *ein Glückskind* — a lucky child — and that it was this belief that gave her hope during her time in the camps. Have you, or anyone you know, ever experienced a seemingly baseless faith in something, only to discover later its great importance?

4. The liquidation of the *Arbeitslager* (labor camp), when Ucek and Zarenka are taken from Thomas's family, is a defining moment for Thomas, and one of the few horrors that is never erased from his memory. Before he is taken as well, Thomas declares to the commandant, "Captain, I can work!" Just nine years old at the time, Thomas shows astounding courage. Do you think that in similar circumstances you would have had the fortitude that young Thomas demonstrates so many times? What do you think made him step forward and say this? Was it chance or something more?

5. Upon his arrival in the Auschwitz barracks, Thomas sees the Kapos beat and murder an inmate named Spiegel as payback for his disloyalty to one of them in Kielce. Thomas wonders whether it occurs to the Kapos that they are no different from Spiegel, for as he had denounced one of them to save himself in the ghetto so had they become Kapos to survive in the camps. He writes, "Had they not ended up in the camps, they probably would have remained decent human beings. What is it in the human character that gives some individuals the moral strength not to sacrifice their decency and

dignity, regardless of the cost to themselves, whereas others become murderously ruthless in the hope of ensuring their own survival?" How would you answer this question?

6. When Thomas is in the United States, he reflects: "I doubt that we would have been able to preserve our sanity had we remained consumed by hatred for the rest of our lives." Do you think you could be as forgiving in such a situation? How do you think Thomas and his mother managed to let go of their anger?

7. *A Lucky Child* is written with a surprisingly unsentimental tone that Buergenthal attributes to the many years that have passed since he was a child of the camps. This lack of sentimentality is one of the facets of the story that sets it apart from other Holocaust memoirs. Did it unsettle you? Did you find that the tone of Buergenthal's writing made it easier or somehow more difficult for you to read about the horrors he experienced?